PRAISE FOR TEACH, BREATHE, LEARN

"Now is the time to transform our educational system for the sake of our children. We need to think outside the box and embrace new approaches that can draw out our deep inner resources. Mindfulness offers a way to tap into the inner resilience, focus and well-being that are already inside us. *Teach, Breathe, Learn* is a key that unlocks this inner potential. This book makes mindfulness accessible for teachers everywhere and is a great resource for sharing mindfulness with young people. It is a helpful tool for parents and educators of all backgrounds. As an accomplished international educator and dedicated mindfulness practitioner, Meena Srinivasan brings these two worlds together in this compelling book, showing how to embed mindfulness into teaching and life. Meena's current work implementing Social Emotional Learning in the Oakland public school district embodies her commitment to transforming our nation's education system from the inside out."
—Congressman Tim Ryan, *A Mindful Nation*

"Completely inspiring. Meena Srinivasan addresses what mindfulness training is, why it matters, and how to bring it to the classroom. What a smart, compelling read! I want to run out and buy *Teach, Breathe, Learn* for every teacher I know."
—Kathryn Lee, project director of RULER for Families,
Yale Center for Emotional Intelligence

"Meena Srinivasan offers an inspiring vision of what a truly mindful education can look like. Her eloquent personal anecdotes and lesson plans are a guide into a new and transformative educational paradigm."
—Daniel Rechtschaffen, MFT, *The Way of Mindful Education*

"*Teach, Breathe, Learn* provides valuable insights and practical tips for educators. It is a wonderful toolbox, ideal for both professional and personal development."
—Lilian Cheung, DSc, RD, coauthor, *Savor*

"Clear, honest, and heartfelt, *Teach, Breathe, Learn* is a book by a truly exceptional teacher. It addresses the day-to-day realities of classroom teaching and offers teachers very practical ways to share specific skills to help students cultivate inner and outer peace throughout their school day, and in their lives beyond the classroom."
—Amy Saltzman MD, *A Still Quiet Place*

"Meena Srinivasan's experienced and kind voice, her respect for her colleagues, and her inclusion of the voices of her students demonstrates a lived understanding of the interconnection that mindfulness reveals. This is a careful and comprehensive guide to mindful teaching and learning."
—Mirabai Bush, *Contemplative Practices in Higher Education*

"*Teach, Breathe, Learn* is a very readable, insightful book, filled with wisdom, that makes crystal clear the power of mindfulness in the classroom and how it can transform students' lives."
—Theo Koffler, founder, Mindfulness Without Borders

"Meena Srinivasan's authentic teacher's voice narrates her journey into mindfulness both in and out of the classroom. *Teach, Breathe, Learn* is a delicious masala of recipes for any educator interested in mapping their own journey into mindfulness."
—Lauren Alderfer, PhD, *Mindful Monkey, Happy Panda*

"*Teach, Breathe, Learn* provides an intimate look into the life and teaching of an experienced mindfulness practitioner. Meena Srinivasan beautifully describes developing and sharing mindfulness lessons with students and teachers and using these same mindfulness practices in her own life."
—Richard Brady, president, Mindfulness in Education Network

"This truly is authentic social and emotional learning in action! Srinivasan combines personal mindfulness practice with her skills as a gifted classroom teacher to produce a model for all who seek to explore and develop mindfulness in education."
—Kevin Hawkins, middle school principal, International School of Prague

"This book offers a model of teaching that can be embraced by any teacher ready to commit to a journey of self-awareness, mindfulness, and authenticity. Meena's students demonstrate, in their own words, what it means to be human and to live with gratitude and compassion."
—Prajna Hallstrom, founder of the Karuna School: A High School for Peace

"A must-have for mindful teachers. *Teach, Breathe, Learn* is chock-full of useful resources. It shows why and how mental fitness enhances teaching and increases learning. Srinivasan is a teachers' teacher, and her authentic and authoritative voice communicates practical wisdom with gentleness and grace."
—Deborah Schoeberlein David, MEd, *Mindful Teaching and Teaching Mindfulness*

"Meena Srinivasan shares detailed and inspirational narratives and reflections on her careful approach to support the social, emotional and moral development of her students. She provides curricular materials and wise guidance for anyone wishing to bring mindfulness into the lives of students."
—Irene McHenry, PhD, Executive Director, Friends Council on Education

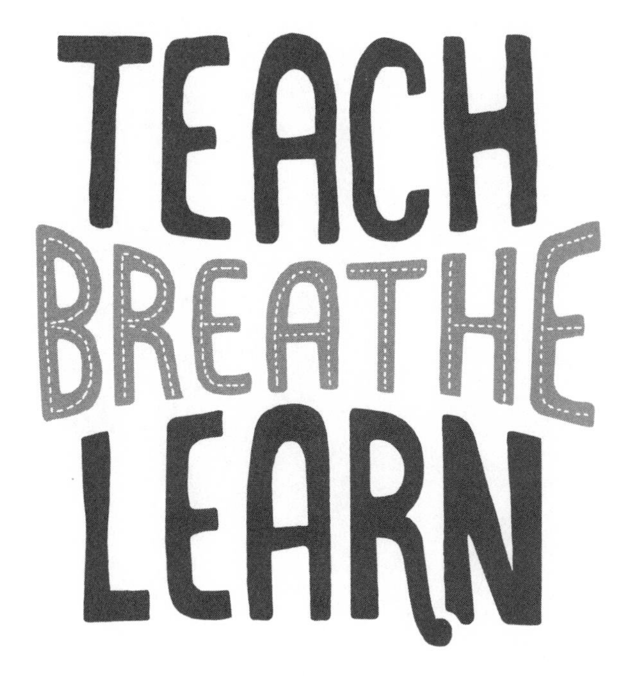
TEACH
BREATHE
LEARN

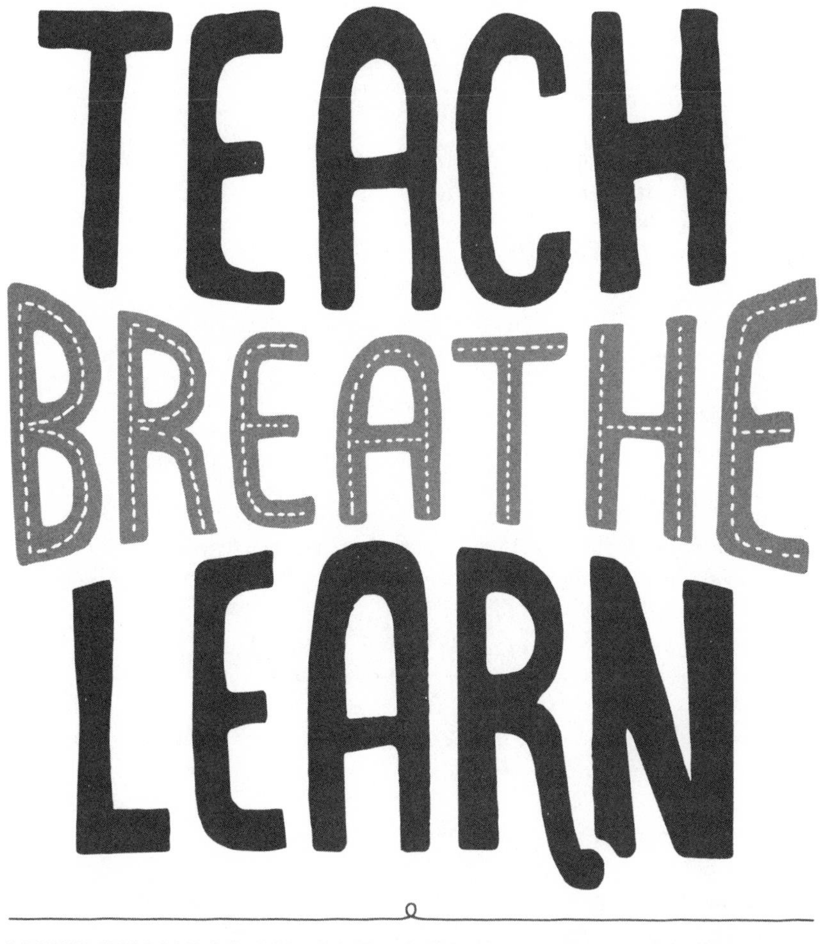

MINDFULNESS IN AND OUT OF THE CLASSROOM

MEENA SRINIVASAN

PARALLAX
PRESS

Berkeley, California

Parallax Press
P.O. Box 7355
Berkeley, California 94707

Parallax Press is the publishing division of the Unified Buddhist Church, Inc.

Printed in the United States of America

Edited by Hisae Matsuda
Cover and text design by Debbie Berne

Students and their families have granted permission for their quotes and voices to appear in this book. In some cases names have been changed, and last names of students are not used to protect their identity as minors.

Library of Congress Cataloging-in-Publication Data
Srinivasan, Meena.
Teach, breathe, learn : mindfulness in and out of the classroom / Meena Srinivasan.
pages cm
ISBN 978-1-937006-74-7 (paperback)
1. Attention--Study and teaching. 2. Awareness--Study and teaching. 3. Emotions and cognition. 4. Learning, Psychology of. 5. Mindfulness-based cognitive therapy. I. Title.
LB1065.S73 2014
370.15'23--dc23

2014015237

3 4 5 6 / 18 17 16 15

In memory of Tom Little, founding teacher and director of Park Day School, the birthplace of mindful schools. May Tom's commitment to bringing mindfulness into education continue through the countless lives he's touched.

To all my students—you are my greatest teachers.

You can count the seeds in an apple, but you can't count the apples in a seed. When you teach, you never know how many lives you will influence . . . you are teaching for eternity.

—Karen Jensen

CONTENTS

FOREWORD

HAPPY TEACHERS CHANGE THE WORLD. Each of us can learn to cultivate and grow our joy; this is the gift and the invitation of mindfulness. We don't need more time in our day to be mindful. We can simply do the things we usually do, but with deepening awareness, relaxation and joy. We can't transmit mindfulness if we don't embody it first.

The most important thing we can offer others is our own happiness and peace. We can do this, first, by bringing greater mindfulness and ease into our own daily lives and, second, by sharing these qualities with our students and colleagues. This book, by a master teacher, shows us how.

Teach, Breathe, Learn is a practical guide to help educators find their own unique path to deeper fulfillment and efficacy in their own lives and in their work. Meena is a precious ambassador of mindfulness, concretely showing us how to bring mindfulness to the 'front lines' of the classroom, the staffroom, and everywhere throughout our day.

The wisdom in this book is grounded in Meena's personal experience of applying mindfulness and compassion to respond rather than react to situations, in order to nurture what is best in us and in our students, and in order to skillfully take care of difficult moments.

These teachings are of a secular nature, reflecting the innate human qualities of mindfulness and compassion. The practices and curriculum in this book are the very foundations of creating true peace in the world. They are a powerful peace education that our students, educators, families and society desperately need. I am deeply pleased that such a resource will now be available for educators and caregivers.

Thich Nhat Hanh
Plum Village, France, 2014

INTRODUCTION

THERE IS MORE awareness than ever about the need for mindfulness in education. In this era of information technology, there are changing demands on teachers, students, support staff, and parents. Mindfulness practices can help nourish harmony and happiness for both adults and children, improve cognitive functions, and raise performance in the classroom and extracurricular activities, including sports.

Over ten years ago, after I offered a ten-week course to the teachers at the American Embassy School in New Delhi, a group that met every week as a mindfulness support group. The course emphasized that "happy teachers can change the world" and included sessions not only for the teachers' social, emotional, and spiritual well-being but also with regard to what they could share with their students. There were sessions on awareness of breath, body, feelings, the brain, and the mind; the building of the school as a community, including conflict resolution methods such as deep listening and compassionate speech; mindfulness practices for everyday activities such as eating, walking, and communicating; and some specific practices for children. A few years after we started the program, Meena

Srinivasan joined the school as a teacher. Her high level of motivation and enthusiasm brought a new energy into the group.

Meena instituted a number of innovations and projects into her classroom, many of which are documented in this book. We are lucky to have the valuable collation of her direct experiences from the classroom as well as her lesson planning and practice guidelines for bringing mindfulness into the lives of both adults and young people.

Through her heartfelt enthusiasm and her commitment to the practices she found so useful for herself and her students, Meena has inspired many other educators and become a driving force for the Mindfulness in Education movement. Her perspective and experience in societies as diverse as India, Brazil, and the United States underline the universality of the practices. I'm confident her work will inspire educators to introduce mindfulness practices in their teaching and in their lives.

—*Shantum Seth*

"In basketball—as in life—true joy comes from being fully present in each and every moment, not just when things are going your way. Of course, it's no accident that things are more likely to go your way when you stop worrying about whether you're going to win or lose and focus your full attention on what's happening right this moment. Like life, basketball is messy and unpredictable. It has its way with you, no matter how hard you try to control it. The trick is to experience each moment with a clear mind and open heart. When you do that, the game—and life—will take care of itself."

—**PHIL JACKSON,** *Sacred Hoops: Spiritual Lessons of a Hardwood Warrior*

"Mindfulness is not taking stuff in the way you see it first. First you take a deep breath in and think about how you may have misunderstood it. To me, mindfulness means thinking of all the possibilities of other ways to see it, and thinking before you act. It is important to water your helpful seeds because if you keep watering your unhelpful seeds and others' unhelpful seeds, eventually it becomes so natural to you that you can't water any helpful seeds."

—**BRAELYN,** age 12

"I think the word mindfulness is sort of a compound word. Mind + full + ness. I think it means full of kindness and care toward others. It means 'be kind,' 'care for others,' and 'be a good person' to me."

—**JI WON**, age 10

PART I

PRACTICING MINDFULNESS

CHAPTER ONE

WHAT IS MINDFULNESS?

I've come to the frightening conclusion that I am the decisive element in the classroom. It's my daily mood that makes the weather.
—HAIM GINOTT [1]

MINDFULNESS IS A WAY OF BEING, a practice we can engage in. It's not an abstract state; it's a kind, curious, nonjudgmental awareness that we try to bring to each moment. Before we can share mindfulness with our students we need an experiential understanding of mindfulness from our own practice. Once we begin to develop our own practice, we will see how it impacts our classroom and our relationships with others. With some daily and consistent practice, the practice of mindfulness can bring more awareness, love, and resilience to our daily lives.

As you practice, the most important mantra is "Be kind and gentle to yourself." I inherited my parents' intense immigrant work ethic. Growing up, I was constantly reminded that my father came to the United States in 1969 with less than $200 in his pocket but with a strong commitment to succeed. When I began my mindfulness practice, I went about it in the same driven way I went about studying in high school and would get upset when I was unmindful. I soon realized that there is no end goal in mindfulness; it is a continual journey towards greater awareness and understanding.

Three minutes . . .

That's the only time I had in between classes, before the next bell, at my school in New Delhi, India. Like most teachers, I barely had enough time to use the bathroom during the school day. In the rush to duck out and return before the next class began, I used the girls' bathroom instead of the staff bathroom. Inside the stall, I quickly began going over my lesson for the next period in my mind while sitting on the toilet. Suddenly, I heard the door bang open. "Watch out, Ms. Srinivasan is in a *really* bad mood today—class sucked!" It was a group of girls from my last-period tenth-grade history class. My heart sank as I intently listened to the girls detail my foul mood. Sure, I was upset that my students were talking about me, but I was even more upset because they were right: I was stressed out and miserable and had no idea what to do about it. It was September 2006, my first month of teaching at a new school. My textbooks still hadn't arrived and I was completely overwhelmed and exhausted. In that moment on the toilet, I realized that if I woke up grumpy, I'd pass that grumpiness on to my students, which really only made me *more* grumpy! But without any strategies to manage stress and work with my emotions in a skillful way, the climate of my classroom suffered.

In a flash I learned that my emotional state is transmitted to my students regardless of the lesson I'm teaching. I knew that a lesson absent of authentic, heartful interaction, however instructionally sound, would never create the connected, innovative, and loving classroom I had dreamed of. The demands placed on me to deliver high-quality instruction while covering massive amounts of content were immense. I felt empty. I was at the start of my career, but I already felt emotionally exhausted and incredibly tired from teaching. Even though I had studied at some of the best educational institutions in the world, I came to my profession with no training in how to manage stress or cultivate joy, happiness, and resilience. Particularly in my role as a teacher, interacting with hundreds of young people on a daily basis, I had no ability to help my students learn how to work with difficulties or feel at peace—how could I teach them these most important life skills if I didn't have them myself?

Compounding my increasing stress, constant security alerts had consumed me in fear. New Delhi had become the site of numerous bomb blasts fueled by fundamentalist terrorism. In the course of one month there were five deadly attacks that injured more than a hundred people and killed close to twenty-five, causing our school to cancel all field trips for the semester. We were living under lockdown.

With this backdrop, I was desperate for a sense of harmony and stillness. So, with a hopeful heart, I traveled all the way across Delhi after a long school day to hear a talk by a visiting peace activist at Gandhi Smriti, formerly the home of the great Mahatma Gandhi and now a museum dedicated to his life and work. The speaker was a Vietnamese Zen master named Thich Nhat Hanh. He had come to Gandhi Smriti to honor Mahatma Gandhi's commitment to nonviolent societal transformation. In a soft voice, he encouraged the audience to find peace within themselves by tuning into their own breathing, their bodies, and minds. In a matter of minutes, this tiny Vietnamese monk's simple instructions on bringing awareness to my breathing quickly brought me to a profound sense of calm and peace inside of myself that I had only ever touched before after a lengthy yoga practice. Deeply inspired by this experience, I decided to attend a retreat with him and the monks and nuns of his monastery. They held the retreat, "Towards a Compassionate and Healthy Society," in Northern India and trained more than 500 educators in mindful awareness. The aim of the retreat was to help teachers transform their own lives using the energy of mindfulness as a step toward transforming classrooms into communities of peace and compassion. It was exactly what I was looking for.

This retreat was transformational—for both my teaching practice and my own personal spiritual journey. Through mindfulness, I've learned how to be the strong yet kind teacher that I know my students deserve. My classroom atmosphere has changed for the better. My students are less stressed and I am too! I've always felt that teachers are a vital link in helping individuals realize Gandhi's vision that "if we could change ourselves, the tendencies in the world would also change"; this is why I teach—to touch lives and help make the world a better place in some small way.

For me, teaching began as a sacred task, but with the demands of covering curriculum and supervising children, I forgot my original aspirations. Mindfulness helped reawaken the light inside myself and I came to see how mindfulness, this kind awareness of what's happening in the present moment inside of us and around us, can be a powerful tool to promote well-being in my entire school community. Seeing this potential for positive transformation, I committed myself to integrating mindfulness into all aspects of my life. Eventually, after a few years of regular mindfulness practice, I embarked on a year-long experiment in which I documented the sharing of mindfulness with my students in a blog: *A Year of Mindfulness in the Classroom.* This book, *Teach, Breathe, Learn,* includes the insights I discovered during that endeavor. It is my journey to mindfulness as a classroom teacher. And in this guide you hold lessons learned, lessons taught, and reflections from my students and teaching colleagues. While my mindfulness teaching has been influenced by Thich Nhat Hanh and others from various traditions, the contents of this book are designed for anyone and everyone who wants to work with children more effectively and joyfully.

I hadn't always been always on track to become a teacher. While in college, I had no intentions of becoming an educator. I was, in fact, laser-focused on developing my career as a journalist. I worked as an associate producer for an NBC affiliate news station while going to school full time and held internships at major news outlets. Going into my senior year, I already had a job lined up at ABC network's hard-news division in New York City. Everything in my life was about building a future and working at a hectic pace, but never about having the time to stop and be in the present moment. To bolster my journalism skills, during winter break I held a policy internship in Washington, DC, where I was encouraged by the late journalist George Liston Seay to go abroad before diving into my career with full force. I put ABC News on hold. Instead of moving to New York City after graduation, I spent a year teaching at an international school in Brazil.

In Brazil, the universe breathed a new purpose into me. At last, I had the time to stop and reflect, and there, I could connect with my true self. I began an inner journey while reading Parker Palmer's *The Courage to Teach*.[2] The book encouraged me to connect my heart to my work, to teach as a spiritual practice. I fell in love with classroom teaching—nothing else had ever felt so right before.

But after a year of teaching, I wasn't quite ready to leave my journalism career behind, so I left Brazil for New York to work at ABC News as planned. What had once felt like my path now felt like a dead end. I missed teaching, and my life in New York just felt wrong to me, as if I wasn't where I was meant to be. In Parker Palmer's *Let Your Life Speak: Listening for the Voice of Vocation*, the author advises that before we can tell our life what we want to do with it, we must first listen to our life telling us who we are. Palmer writes, "Our deepest calling is to grow into our own authentic selfhood, whether or not it conforms to some image of who we ought to be. As we do so, we will not only find the joy that every human being seeks—we will also find our path of authentic service in the world."[3] Despite my focus on journalism, my life was telling me that I am, in fact, an educator at heart.

When I started daydreaming about creating lesson plans based on our news stories, I knew I had to return to the classroom—I became sure that teaching was my calling. In fact, it was calling me! I moved to Oakland, California, where I taught at a private high school while getting my teaching credential and then my master's in education at Berkeley. After graduate school, I took my career path to India to explore my ancestral homeland and teach at an international school in New Delhi. It was there that I began to explore teaching as a mindful practice, prompted by those three minutes in the bathroom overhearing my students complaining about my mood.

I studied mindfulness with one of Thich Nhat Hanh's students, Shantum Seth. His organization, Ahimsa Trust, has brought mindfulness to countless Indian teachers. Seeing how beneficial mindfulness was to my own teaching practice, I dedicated myself to sharing it with other educators. Over the years, through Shantum's mentorship and guidance, I've trained and taught other teachers in mindfulness and I've had the opportunity to share mindfulness with many communities in South Asia, including preservice teachers in the northeastern Indian state of Sikkim, South Indian Dalit children, and educators in Bhutan.*

After five years of teaching in India, I returned to the United States to continue teaching and sharing the lessons of

* Dalit is a self-referential Marathi term implying "those who have been oppressed by those above." In the traditional Indian caste system, it refers to a member of the lowest caste.

mindfulness with others, and I'm now tasked with implementing social-emotional learning throughout a large, urban public-school district in the San Francisco Bay Area. In my decade as an educator, I feel truly blessed to have worked in a variety of contexts, from high-powered international schools in India and Brazil to a leading college preparatory and progressive school in the United States. In spite of the differences in cultural and educational environments, I've seen how the principles of mindfulness beneficially transform teacher practice and classroom climate. This is because, regardless of background and setting, we all want to feel connected. Mindfulness enables us to connect deeply with ourselves so in turn we can authentically connect with others.

Beyond the classroom, in my personal life, I've experienced how the practice of using the breath and body as an anchor to come back to myself with compassion and care can help alleviate suffering. A few years ago my mother was diagnosed with a severe lung disease; in less than a year she lost more than half of her lung capacity and had to go on supplemental oxygen. It was a stressful period of my life; soon after my mother's diagnosis I had to make my big move back to the United States from India. Within months, doctors informed my family that my mother's only hope for survival was a double lung transplant. It was a scary time. I had only recently discovered the power of my own breath, and my mother, the one who breathed for me when I was in her womb, the one who brought me the breath of life, was now quickly losing her own ability to breathe. During the months in which we waited for an organ donor, I'd remind myself that in a very real way my mother genetically lives inside me; somehow when

I breathe, she breathes too. So with each mindful breath, I sent her love and worked with my fear and sadness about her condition. Being able to soothe and comfort myself while resting in acceptance of my mother's sickness helped me manage an incredibly difficult situation that I had previously had no way of handling. Mindfulness practice had also given me the tools to really be present with my mother in a way I wasn't capable of being before. Thankfully, my mother eventually received a donor and now, more than a year after her successful double lung transplant, she's a walking miracle of medicine. While I'm grateful for my mother's new lease on life, I'm also more aware of the impermanent nature of all things. Mindfulness enables me to fully savor and cherish the time I have with her.

Life is precious, and mindfulness gives us the tools to live deeply, to connect authentically, and to open our hearts fully. An *experiential* understanding of mindfulness is important for bringing mindfulness practice into the classroom effectively. Providing the necessary rationale is also important. Students, parents, and the larger community need to know about the benefits associated with engaging in mindfulness practices—how it will benefit them and what research says about the effects of practice on academic, social, and emotional learning. Most educational settings will only support initiatives that are research-based, and the good news is this: the science behind mindfulness is expanding daily. Studies with K–12 students demonstrate "improvements in working memory, attention, academic skills, social skills, emotional regulation, and self-esteem, as well as self-reported improvements in mood and decreases in anxiety, stress, and fatigue." They also show that mindfulness training "can increase teachers' sense of well-being and teaching self-efficacy, as well as their ability to manage classroom behavior and establish and maintain supportive relationships with students."[4]

Although rigorous scientific research findings are of course important, many people find their own experiential results of dedicated practice to be the most convincing proof that such practices are worthwhile. For them, the deep sense of presence and resilience they gain is far more powerful than the measureable results of mindfulness. It is this "heartfulness" that teachers then transmit to their students.*

Students are reflections of their teachers, and the most important teachings we as teachers offer transcend academic skills and the acquisition of knowledge. Before teaching content, we must create a learning environment conducive to education. This begins by cultivating an inner sense of boundless love, so that we can receive students with warmth and create a classroom filled with peace. Striving to embody the practice by being the change is what will ultimately transform education.

It's now the spring of 2013, and I tap a bell of mindfulness in a California classroom of boisterous sixth graders. I've rushed in from lunch duty, my mind everywhere, my thoughts scattered. In this one simple sound, we are brought back together, in this space, in each breath we take, in the silence. In one minute, we've gone from chaos to calm, and we are all ready for the lesson to begin . . .

---

* The Sanskrit root, *cit*, refers to the mind, consciousness, and heart, and it is the author's understanding that an experience of mindfulness is one that occurs with a deep connection of heart. In several languages, the word for mind and heart are the same.

> I like the mind-connected-to-the-body method where we practice breathing mindfully to make sure we are fully present. We do it almost every day before Meena's humanities class and I think it really helps with schoolwork and focusing in class.
>
> —**JESSE**, age 11

Mindfulness is energy we cultivate through kind, present-moment awareness. It involves the practice of coming back to the peaceful, compassionate space we all have inside ourselves with curiosity and without judgment. When we come back to this space repeatedly, it grows. The mind is like a muscle—the more it lies in certain states, the more it will seek them. Mindfulness is a way of training our minds through intentional awareness so that they stay in a more peaceful and compassionate state.

The more we practice coming back to the present with kind awareness the easier it is to actually be present—a vital quality for educators! Except perhaps for surgeons, teachers make more decisions than any other professional during the course of the workday, and the demands of the classroom require us to be able to have simultaneously both expansive and focused attention. I've found that by just relaxing into the present moment with mindfulness, I can better understand the children and the atmosphere so I can make decisions more skillfully. For example, when I'm having a particularly challenging situation with a student, if I pause for an instant and go to my breath, I can quickly ease my feelings of anger and respond to the situation in a more loving and understanding way.

> Good teachers share one trait: they are truly present in the classroom, deeply engaged with their students and their subject. . . . [They] are able to weave a complex web of connections among themselves, their subjects, and their students, so that their students can learn to weave

a world for themselves. The connections made by good teachers are held not in their methods but in their hearts.

—PARKER PALMER[5]

Mindfulness enables us to be more responsive and less reactive. My very first "Wow, this mindfulness stuff really works!" classroom moment was very powerful. I was teaching a middle school academic support class at an international school in New Delhi, India. My class had students from all over the world, all of them had varying special needs, and I was charged with supporting all of them. When I shared with my students that we were hiring an instructional assistant to help provide more support for our class, one of my beautiful American boys yelped, "I hope it's not an Indian!" In that moment my heart sank. I was one of the few teachers of color at the international school and the only expat of Indian origin. I felt extremely hurt by his comment, and feelings of anger and sadness bubbled inside of me. The premindfulness me would have snapped at him that his comment was unacceptable, but now, because of my mindfulness practice, I engaged in emotional self-regulation. Recognizing my feelings as they arose within me, I paused and took a breath, and instead of shutting my student down I politely asked him why he didn't want an Indian instructional assistant. He explained that he found it very difficult to understand Indian accents and this made it hard for him to learn. As he spoke, I realized he had no intention of hurting my feelings as someone with an Indian heritage; instead I saw a young boy who had difficulty learning, a boy who hadn't chosen to be in India, a boy who was brought there because of his father's job—a boy who felt frustrated and needed my love and acknowledgment of his feelings. From that moment forward, I made it my policy to always engage my students in dialogue in order to really understand them. I realized that only when I understood them could I truly teach them.

TEACHER RESPONSES TO MINDFULNESS

I'd also like to share some reflections on mindfulness from some of my teaching colleagues who participated in a mindfulness practice group with me. I've included their thoughts here so you can connect with other teacher voices on the power and potential of mindfulness.

> Mindfulness for me is the practice of acceptance of my place on the path to consciousness and an awareness of self in reference to the rest of existence.
>
> With my fourth graders, I've found myself being patient and compassionate in new ways and looking for ways to relieve the stressful events of their lives. One example is having some of the kids look at the reasons they played soccer. As a team, we had all the soccer players come together to talk about helping each other out. When kids in the class began to form exclusive cliques in the second semester, I would sit down with them as a group and talk about friendship and inclusiveness as a choice. I also changed the way I grouped kids for collaborative efforts. I tried to include groups that would hopefully open kids up to new possibilities in relationships.
>
> From the practice I've gained a recognition of myself on the journey; I've seen my patience, compassion, and thoughtfulness growing. Mindfulness gives students another set of tools to tap into their true intention for their lives and their connection to the larger community and world. Kids can get swept away in "group think," and any practice of mindfulness in education brings them back, even if only for a few moments, to their own center. It gives them a moment away from the concerns they have about how others perceive them or how they fit in and gives them space inside for themselves . . . their true selves. Rare for middle school kids.
>
> —**MICHAEL CITRINO,** middle school art teacher, American Embassy School, New Delhi

Mindfulness connects my mind and body with an awareness of the present moment. Mindfulness gives me the space to be a gentle, inquisitive, nonjudgmental observer even in times of great personal discomfort. Mindfulness means less reactivity in my life and more genuine listening.

The practice helps me in very practical ways with pacing and managing work fatigue. Also, it is the regular practice that nurtures peace within me so that I can truly have peace to offer others.

In my fourth-grade classroom, I implemented a mindfulness bell practice with students by inviting the bell every thirty minutes. It was amazing how quickly we all came to crave that regular interval for returning to our true selves. For me as a teacher, it became a time that I touched my inner wisdom about what was really needed for my students at that exact moment. My students recognized the practice as supporting their focus, learning, and inner calm. Once, when I was away from my classroom for a weeklong workshop, I found myself missing the mindfulness bell desperately. I was longing for those regular intervals of peace. Without it, I felt like I was going through the days without ever touching peace.

I think that mindfulness practices have a lot to offer students in the area of focus and learning. We get bombarded with so much information and so many tasks to complete that the ability to focus on the here and now is important in the arena of education. I think that mindfulness practices can also support students in coping with emotional distress, experiencing and cultivating inner peace. Cultivating inner peace among the members of an educational institution can have a profound and far-reaching impact on the learning environment and larger community.

—**KATHY,** fourth-grade teacher, American Embassy School, New Delhi

~

Mindfulness has been particularly helpful in dealing with trying situations with my students. There will always be students who "push my buttons" in some way, and I think it has been my goal to find alternative ways of working with those students so that they learn from the situation and still feel nurtured and loved. My knee-jerk reactions of the past come less frequently as I've committed to practice breathing when something challenging arises in the classroom. In addition to the more conversational responses I've learned to use with students, I've also discovered the technique of not responding at all. For some reason, I've become less reactionary, and there are many times that I don't respond because nothing would be gained by it and because it really isn't that big of a deal anyway. Many more things just "roll off my back" that may have triggered a reaction from me in the past. This is an ongoing, mindful intent for me and I am constantly working/playing with it, but I am encouraged by the process/progress.

In addition to using mindfulness myself, I use the mindfulness bell in the classroom with students. I start by just offering it as a reminder to relax and refocus so that they have a more rewarding and successful experience when they return to their work. When the opportunity arises, I also talk with students about the value of taking a breath in difficult situations so that they can make better choices.

—**BARBARA HEGRANES,** middle school math teacher, American Embassy School, New Delhi

CHAPTER TWO

EVERY BREATH COUNTS

Your breath is your best friend.
—PROFESSOR RAMCHANDRA GANDHI

PROFESSOR RAMCHANDRA GANDHI was one of India's brightest contemporary philosophers and original thinkers. Not only was he the grandson of Mahatma Gandhi, but he was an Oxford-trained philosopher who taught at some of India's most prestigious educational institutions, including Rabindranath Tagore's famed school, Shantiniketan. We met within days of my arrival to New Delhi, and to me it felt as if our meeting were divinely ordained. My short time under his tutelage was a beautiful blend of the spirit and engagement with ideas that matter, and I feel blessed to have developed a close connection with him. Sadly, he passed away nine months after we met, but after his death I felt even closer to him. "Your breath is your best friend," was one of the many pithy lessons Professor Gandhi imparted; it was only when I connected with Thich Nhat Hanh's mindfulness teachings that I truly understood what he meant.

Your breath is always with you. Observing the breath is one of the easiest, simplest ways to start practicing mindfulness. Mindful breathing can be done anytime, anywhere. By bringing awareness to your breathing, you can gently bring a wandering mind back to the present moment. You can also use the practice of reciting a *gatha*, which is a short insightful verse from the Zen tradition, as you mindfully breathe to calm yourself. Saying these positive affirmations to yourself can help you take a more peaceful, positive outlook on things.

If we are to truly pay attention to taking care of our spirits and bodies, then starting our days by switching off the To Do list and practicing mindful breathing is a wonderful way to fill up our gas tanks. When practicing mindful breathing, I usually place my hand on my abdomen or chest so I can feel my body expand and contract with my breaths. I make sure my back is straight but at ease and either sit on a comfortable cushion on the floor with my knees below my diaphragm or in a chair with my feet grounded to the floor. My husband, Chihiro, and I have created a small but sacred breathing space in our home with candles and meaningful quotes around us to inspire us as we begin to practice breathing together. We usually close our eyes, but if you feel more comfortable with your eyes open you can maintain a soft focus as you gaze. We live very close to a beautiful marina; sometimes we'll practice there and then we keep our eyes open and take in the view! Try practicing in a variety of settings and find what works best for you.

When I sit in my breathing space in the morning, the practice spills into the rest of the day. It may be easiest to start with five minutes and gradually increase your practice by five minutes each week. Ideally, spending thirty to forty-five minutes is most beneficial, but given our many commitments, that may not be possible. Even if you can breathe mindfully for only ten to fifteen minutes at a time, you can take time throughout the day to breathe. Whenever you are in line somewhere, for example while waiting to use the photocopy machine, at the coffee shop, or at a stoplight, use this time to come back to yourself and practice mindful breathing.

Throughout the day you can check in and notice if your breath is short or long, shallow or deep. When you practice mindful

Daily Sitting Practice

Committing to a daily sitting practice is necessary to cultivate mindfulness and help it grow. A formal sitting practice contributes to not only greater awareness of thoughts, emotions, and sensations throughout your day, but it also helps you let go of judging all of your experiences as good or bad.

Once you are comfortable with practicing mindfulness of the breath, you can practice mindfulness of physical sensations in your body, sound, thoughts, or emotions. Seeing our thoughts as *clouds in the sky* is a common metaphor used to help us not get caught in endless thinking when sitting. Every time you observe a thought, you place it on a cloud in the sky and watch it move across the sky. You are aware of the thought but you don't get caught in it. You simply take note of it and let it float away.

I find it helpful to set an intention before I begin to get grounded into my sit. I do this to remind myself why I make this intentional time to be with myself every day. An intention can be as simple as "I intend to be peaceful" or "I intend to be happy." For a few years my intention was "I intend to release all that is not love and generosity from my heart." When my mom was sick it was "I intend to have courage." An intention is not a goal you set out to measure or achieve; rather it's an expression of a heartfelt commitment to your own well-being.

breathing, you can easily trigger your parasympathetic nervous system, which corresponds to a more relaxed state of body and mind. I had a student notice that her breath was short and shallow during a math test, and she instantly began practicing mindful breathing to calm herself down so she could better focus on her test. I've also noticed that with continued practice I'm able to momentarily suspend my thinking when I focus on the sensations of mindful breathing and am fully present to each inhalation and exhalation. For someone with a busy, racing mind, these moments of rest are deeply relaxing and rejuvenating.

MINDFUL CLASSROOM PREP

Often during my prep periods I'd have a lot of items to organize for my lessons. Instead of focusing on how I have so many pieces of construction paper to cut for a class activity or supply boxes to organize, I'd revel in how I could breathe while getting these supplies together for my lesson. I'd sit at the large paper cutter and breathe deeply each time I cut a piece of paper. Similarly, when I had to clean my classroom at the end of the day or organize my class books I'd approach it as an opportunity to practice mindful breathing and with each sweep or swoop of the hand I'd breathe deeply.

GATHAS

Often when I wish to cultivate a positive state with my students I use this gatha:

Breathing in, I feel happy.
Breathing out, I smile to my happiness.

First I try to connect with their smiling faces, their enthusiasm and laughter. (Watching students during recess or lunch duty or as they arrive at school can be a perfect time to practice this exercise.) Their fresh smiles and laughter remind me to connect with that same freshness within myself throughout the day. Using my breath as a guide, I silently say to myself as I breathe: "Breathing in, I feel happy. Breathing out, I smile to my happiness." I exchange the word "happy" with "joy," "freshness," and "peace."

Breathing in, I feel happy.
Breathing out, I smile to my happiness.

Breathing in, I feel fresh.
Breathing out, I smile to my freshness.

Breathing in, I feel peace.
Breathing out, I smile to my peacefulness.

Thich Nhat Hanh's books *Blooming of a Lotus* and *Present Moment, Wonderful Moment* are great resources for gathas and guided meditations. You can even record yourself reading the guided meditations and play them to yourself in the morning before your day begins!

HUGGING MINDFULLY

When Chihiro and I first began living together, we had a really challenging time transitioning once we came home from work. According to my husband, if I come straight home after work instead of going to yoga, I storm in full of "crazy energy" in which I'm focused on getting things done at the sacrifice of being present with him or with what I'm doing. One evening, after a particularly lengthy faculty meeting at school, I raced home and started making dinner at a frenetic pace. Thinking about the next step in preparing our food, I sliced through an eggplant with lightning speed and ended up cutting my finger. Blood spurted all around me, and Chihiro came over to soothe me. While he put pressure on my finger to stop the bleeding, we practiced mindful breathing. As the bleeding subsided and I began to calm down, we decided that from now on when we come home from work, the first thing we would do is give each other a three-breath hug. In doing this, we connect back to our bodies; the practice grounds us as it reminds us how grateful we are to have each other in our lives. When I become a parent, I hope to do the same with my child for as long as she or he will let me!

INVITING A MINDFULNESS BELL

Incorporating a mindfulness bell into your day is also a great strategy to practice mindful breathing. Mindfulness bells are now easily available online or at meditation practice centers. In the Plum Village tradition in which I learned how to use a mindfulness bell, we were taught never to "ring" or "strike" the bell but rather to "invite" the bell because engaging in mindfulness is an invitation to be present. Inviting the bell is in itself a very powerful mindfulness practice. Before using the striker to "invite" the bell, I was instructed to first breathe in and out a few times and then on the third breath I'd send out my breath, my full presence, along with the sound of the bell, while silently chanting: "Body, speech, and mind in perfect oneness, I send my heart along with the sound of the bell. May the hearers awaken from forgetfulness and transcend all anxiety and sorrow." The sound is an invitation to come back to ourselves through mindful breathing. Then before sounding the bell again I'd "wake" it by gently tapping the side of the bell with the striker. After waking the bell, I'd breathe deeply at least one more time and then invite the bell. The gatha for listening to the bell is "Listen, listen, the wonderful sound brings one back to my true home."

In our home we take great pleasure in inviting the bell before our morning sit or before meals. Some of my friends have even instructed their children to invite the bell when there is disharmony in the home. In this way the children partner with their parents in practicing mindfulness, often reminding everyone to take a breath, cultivate calm, and come back to themselves when tensions get high.

You don't need a physical bell to benefit from a mindfulness bell. You can program your phone using a number of meditation apps (one I like to use is the Insight Timer) or your computer using a variety of online mindfulness clocks so that a bell goes off every so often. Whenever you hear the bell you can use this as a reminder to bring awareness to your breathing. I always start my classes by inviting the bell—not only is this a great way to help the children transition to our time together but it also helps *me* cultivate the presence I need to be an effective teacher. Before inviting the bell, I begin by saying to my students, "Okay, your bodies are here, but where is your mind? Is your mind still at lunch? Still at recess? Still in science class?" When my students hear the bell they bring awareness to their breathing, which instantly connects their minds to their bodies. If you are concerned about the implications of using a Tibetan singing bowl or Asian meditation bell, you can use a Latin percussion vibratone or a musical instrument such as a triangle. In some classes I'd have my students rotate as bell masters and a different student would invite the bell to get our class started each day.

The beautiful sunshine, a baby's smile, and the sound of laughter can also serve as mindfulness bells. In short, anything that helps your mind gently come back to your body through conscious breathing is a bell of mindfulness.

> Mindfulness is being present and thoughtful. It's to be living in the moment. Being mindful is to catch yourself when you feel your mind wandering or thinking about things other than what you're supposed to be focusing on. You can come back to your breath to do this. To me, mindfulness means to concentrate in class. Now, whenever I'm in class, I make sure to be present.
>
> —**UMA**, age 11

CHAPTER THREE

EVERY STEP COUNTS

Every journey begins with a single step.

WHEN I FIRST HEARD of Asia's most holy mountain and lake ten years ago, I was living in New York City and the idea of going to Western Tibet seemed like a faraway dream. For thousands of years, Mount Kailash and Lake Mansarovar have played a significant role in the collective consciousness of Hindus, Buddhists, Jains, and Sikhs. In all these spiritual traditions, circumambulating Mount Kailash is said to purify our karma and generate merit in our spiritual path. While I was teaching in India, I was given the opportunity to go on a pilgrimage to these sacred sites. There are few moments in our lives that we never, ever forget; when I first laid eyes on Mount Kailash and Lake Mansarovar, I was consumed with gratitude, bliss, peace, joy, and complete awe. Words and pictures cannot capture the essence, vastness, and spiritual grandeur of this glorious mountain and lake. It takes three days to complete the thirty-two-mile circumambulation of Mount Kailash. The most challenging part of the journey is the Dolma-La Pass, where at 19,500 feet you only have about forty percent of the oxygen you need. At that altitude, every step and breath counts. Earlier that year during Thich Nhat Hanh's visit to India, I had learned how to walk mindfully by coordinating each step with my breath and silently saying a gatha or positive word to myself with each step. It was there in Western Tibet, carrying my own heavy gear without a porter, that I first experienced the power of mindful walking.

As I circumambulated the mountain, I coordinated each step with my breath and a line from my favorite gatha: "I have arrived. I am home. In the here. In the now. I am solid. I am free. In the Ultimate I dwell." "Arrived. Home. Here. Now. Solid. Free. Ultimate. Dwell." During my three-day journey around the mountain, thanks to mindful walking, I was able to manage the high altitude and bathe in the beauty and glory of Kailash. Walking mindfully, I became the first person in my group to complete the entire circuit on foot and I wasn't even tired or sore!

Teaching can often feel like climbing a mountain. In the busyness of the school day, mindful walking is a nourishing practice that can help us set the tone for our classes and our meetings with parents and colleagues. It also strengthens our capacity to be more aware in all parts of our life. Mindful walking involves bringing our full attention to the practice of walking. By also focusing on how each foot lifts up and steps down from your toes to your heel, you can engage fully with the feeling of the soles of your feet as they touch the ground or, as Thich Nhat Hanh says, "kiss the Earth."

I try to walk from the parking lot to my classroom mindfully each morning using words like "joy," "happiness," "peace," or "love" with each step. When I do this, I can quickly shift my state of mind so I arrive at my classroom in a more receptive, positive mood. I also make sure to try to walk certain paths at my school mindfully, like the path from my classroom to the bathroom. Using these transitional times to nourish my peace of mind is a great way to take care of myself during the school day. Mindful walking is a great way to practice mindfulness on the days when you just don't have time to sit.

With limited space at school sites many teachers have to share classrooms. This means you may not have your own space to work in during the school day. When I moved back to the United States from India, I took a job teaching at an independent school in Oakland, California. After having had my own classroom in New Delhi, I found it very challenging to suddenly start sharing my space during the day because I couldn't get my work done when another class was being taught in my room. If I was in the room, even if I wasn't teaching, students would assume I was available for help. Without a staff room at my school, I had no place I could work when my room was being used. I decided that instead of fussing about how I could work during this forty-minute block, I would look at it as a gift—a gift of time during my usually fast-paced school day. I'd spend half the period making copies or doing whatever prep I could do outside of my room and dedicate the rest to mindful walking. I figured this time was best used nourishing myself so I slowly strolled around the neighborhood near my school, communing with the outdoors and taking in mindful breaths with each step. After my sessions of mindful walking, I'd return to campus feeling refreshed, restored, recharged, and ready to teach. On the days when it rained heavily, I wasn't able to take those mindful walks and instead was stuck in the classroom. I noticed how I held some resentment for not being able to completely delve into my work. I realized that taking time to tune into my well-being during those twenty-minute mindful walks enabled me to receive my students in a much more relaxed, kind, and open way. Even taking the time to mindfully walk to the staff bathroom before class could be a quick way to reconnect to my body.

By practicing mindful walking, I give myself a chance to stop, listen, and feel all that's around me, from the breeze on my skin to the rain or sun on my face. Oftentimes I notice beautiful flowers or plants that I usually walk past without knowing they're there!

Bringing greater awareness to everyday activities like walking enhances our ability to be present. It can also be a great way for young people to practice mindfulness if they have difficulty sitting still. In chapter fifteen, I detail how to introduce mindful walking to your students. Once it's an established practice, you can utilize it in a number of ways. I use mindful walking as a strategy to refocus students. Whenever I sense that a student needs a break, is overwhelmed, or is about to get off task, I encourage them to take a mindful walking break. Mindful walking is also a wonderful way to transition to class, create a reflective space for writing assignments, or practice close observation in science or art. Most importantly, when students see you practicing mindful walking on school grounds, it reinforces the practice in their eyes. For example, I shared with students which paths on the school grounds I committed to walking mindfully. Whenever they saw me walking mindfully they would smile and occasionally join me in the practice.

Romi

I saw some butterflies and a cat and I've noticed that when I walked slowly I realized more things that I haven't noticed before like last time I went walking.

FUN

— **ROMI,** age 11

CHAPTER FOUR

DEEP RELAXATION

Mindfulness is paying attention on purpose, non-judgmentally, in the present moment, as if your life depended on it.

—JON KABAT-ZINN

DEEP RELAXATION IS a wonderful self-care practice, especially for those of us who are accustomed to working at a fast, sometimes frenetic pace in our daily lives. The experience of stopping for this short period of rest illustrates how much more effective our working time can be when we listen to the needs of our bodies and minds. After a session of deep relaxation I usually feel refreshed, energized, and rejuvenated. Essentially, it involves consciously relaxing parts of our body. In the lesson plans included in this book, there is a script you can use with students to teach them the skill of deep relaxation too.

You can begin by lying down on your back in a comfortable position. Close your eyes. Bring awareness to your belly and practice a hundred counts of mindful breathing. "Breathing in, I feel my belly rise. Breathing out, I relax my body." To start, I find it helpful to gently place one hand on my belly and another hand on my chest so I can feel my belly and chest rise and fall. Then you can gradually move your attention to different parts of your body. I usually start with my hands and feet and then go from my head downwards focusing on various parts of my body. "Breathing in, I bring awareness to my eyes. Breathing out, I send love to my eyes. Breathing in, I bring awareness to my mouth. Breathing out, I bring love and gratitude to my mouth." I finish with sending love and healing to any part of my body that is suffering. Granting yourself time to truly relax and consciously send love and gratitude to your body is an incredibly nourishing practice.

Last year when I first shared the practice of deep relaxation with my sixth graders, they started a petition and had every class member sign it to request that I teach them deep relaxation every day! We made a compromise that every Friday, last period, they would have the option of doing relaxation before we began our weekly reading workshop. One student shared,

> Before practicing deep relaxation I felt really heavy and I was very worried about several things that were happening at that very moment. During the practice I felt like I was glued to the floor. I felt like I was in heaven. When doing the deep relaxation I felt like just doing deep relaxation for the rest of my life. When I finished, I felt really calm and loose and really, really fresh. I felt much much better. I felt pleased and really thankful.

Practicing in this way, students learn to self-soothe, regulate their behavior, and experience that they can find relief from stressful situations by simply focusing attention on their breath and body. Once they learn how to practice deep relaxation at school, it can become a self-care skill that they can employ throughout their lives. Many students also share that once they've learned it at school they use it at home to help them fall asleep when they have trouble sleeping.

When I first began attending mindfulness retreats I was struck by the heightened awareness that came with consciously being present. For the first time I noticed the songs the birds were singing, the steam coming off of my teacup, and the clouds moving across the sky. Food tasted better, flowers seemed brighter, and life felt richer.

As a result, I carried over this mindfulness practice into my daily life. Now I'm more awake: to the leaves and trees dancing in the wind, the smiles on the train, the beautiful sunsets. Mindfulness creates a sense of wonder I didn't have before—this awe in the beauty of every day life that surrounds me.

In the book *The Miracle of Mindfulness*, the Vietnamese translator Mobi Ho shares a story about how he was once cooking and couldn't seem to find a spoon he just used. As he was frantically searching for the spoon Thich Nhat Hanh walked in and asked, "What are you looking for?" Mobi said he was looking for a spoon. Thich Nhat Hanh smiled and replied, "No you are looking for Mobi."

This story illustrates how easily we get lost when we are not dialed in. I need to intentionally take time to come back to my breath, my body, and my sensations or I feel dispersed and lost. At times life can seem like an endless list of things to do. When we get caught up in the list and are not present for the moment in front of us, the consequence is much more than misplacing a spoon—it's missing out on life.

CHAPTER FIVE

MINDFUL EATING

When we eat food at home, we don't think of what people went through just so we could enjoy our food. When we started eating the orange [during the process of learning mindful eating], I was actually thinking about what these people did, and for the first time in my life I felt as though I was thanking people I don't even know. This helped me realize how fortunate I am. It also made me think how everything we eat and drink starts off as such a little thing and that we are dependent on other people in order to get our supply of food.

—**AKASH, age 15**

THROUGHOUT MY LIFE I've eaten many oranges. While I don't remember the first time I ate an orange, I do remember the first time I ate one mindfully. Native to India, the *mosambi* tastes like an orange but it has a green peel. It was a September Saturday afternoon and along with about one hundred others gathered on the lawn of the India International Center in New Delhi for a talk by Thich Nhat Hanh, I peeled and smelled this citrus fruit as if for the first time. As I slowly savored the fruit, Thich Nhat Hanh asked a number of questions: "Where did this orange come from? How did it get here?" As I meditated in awe on the infinite number of causes and conditions from the seed to the sun to the soil to the farmers to the store that led to this sweet fruit on my tongue, it felt like I was eating an orange for the very first time. Through this experience I realized that, just like the orange, I too have been nurtured by numerous individuals to become who I am today. The more I remember the miracle of the orange, the more I recognize the miracle of my life—this is the ultimate power that lies in mindful eating. It allows us to realize the interconnectedness of all phenomena.

We all have to eat. Yet how many of us are actually present when we are eating and truly tasting our food? Through bringing awareness to our eating we can transform our meals into a very nourishing experience. To practice mindful eating, I try to find a quiet place where I can eat and really be present with my food. First, I breathe mindfully before I begin and take a moment to smell and look deeply at my food. Then, I practice gratitude for the food and all of the elements that created my meal from the sun, rain, and soil to the farmers, cooks, and other people who participated in bringing my meal to the table. Sometimes I'll say the Food Contemplations in the Plum Village tradition.

Plum Village Food Contemplations Practice

This food is the gift of the whole universe: the earth, the sky, the rain, and the sun.

We thank the people who have made this food, especially the farmers, the people at the market, and the cooks.

We only put on our plate as much food as we can eat.

We want to chew the food slowly so that we can enjoy it.

This food gives us energy to practice being more loving and understanding.

We eat this food in order to be healthy and happy, and to love each other as a family.[6]

With each bite I try to taste deeply, savoring the food and chewing slowly at least forty times, placing my utensil down and only lifting it again when I am done swallowing. If my mind wanders, I silently say the name of the food to myself or I say, "nourishing," "gratitude," or simply "thank you."

On days when I don't have meetings, lunch duty, or appointments to work with students, I try to find a quiet, private place to eat my lunch. Before I practiced mindful eating, I'd eat while thinking about my worries, literally consuming my stress. Now, even if I can take fifteen minutes to mindfully eat, it makes a huge difference in my state of mind and gives me a nourishing break in the middle of my day.

Eating is a *very* effective way of introducing mindfulness into your life. I've also found mindful eating to be a great way of helping young people get a better sense of what mindfulness is. An experiment in which I've often engaged my students and fellow educators is this: first take a small piece of food and eat it normally—then try eating it mindfully. Try this with your next meal and take note of how different your experience is when you do this.

Student Reflections on Eating a Chocolate-Covered Berry

The first time I ate the berry I just gobbled it down but the second time, when I savored it, I actually tasted the berry after the chocolate melted in my mouth. The chocolate was dark chocolate and it was smooth when the berry was hard and tasted like strawberry. The second time tasted way better than the first.

—**GAGANA,** age 10

I think eating the berry the second time was a lot better. It tasted better, probably because the second time I observed and thought about the berry a lot more. The first time I thought about it a little but not as deeply. My grandmother always savors everything she eat, probably because when she was little and the war was going on, all she had to eat was potato peels. Now I know why she savors.

—**KATHY,** age 10

The first time I ate it, it was nothing. It was a chocolate. The second time I ate it, I felt the sweetness and I feel grateful for this wonderful piece of chocolate.

—**CHLOE,** age 11

It tasted better. It was more flavorful. I was more mindful of where it came from.

—**JACOB,** age 10

Early on in my teaching of mindfulness, the parent of one of my tenth graders unexpectedly stopped by my classroom after school one day and asked if she could speak with me. I was pleasantly shocked when she said, "Meena, thank you for bringing mindfulness into our home! Last week, Maggie came home and asked if I'd mindfully eat an orange with her. I couldn't believe it! She then shared all of the mindfulness strategies you've been teaching her in class. Now we take time to really be more present with our food and practice gratitude for all the infinite sources involved in each meal—from the sun, to the soil, to the farmers, to the shopkeepers, and the cooks!"

Reflections on Mindful Eating

I ate corn mindfully. When I ate it I was thinking how it got here and how far did it come from now to be in my hands. I was eating it slowly to really get the taste of it. I was also thinking that not every child gets to eat whatever they want or not even get any food. I think that eating mindfully helps us appreciate that we can have food to eat and it helps us to really get the taste of the food that we are eating.

—**DALMA,** age 10

When I eat my dinner mindfully, I can taste the food deeply and clearly. And when you chew the rice well, some sweetness will coming

out and it's delicious. So I think mindfully eating something is like you can enjoy to eat something better than usual and you can also realize how tasty is the food. I think most important thing for eating mindfully is chewing food well. I also aware of mindfully eat something makes you feel happy because you can taste your meal more tasty than usual.
—**RYUJI**, age 11

I ate potatoes with onion soup and I thought of how I got this. Because someone must peel the potato, someone made the onion soup powder, which is a lot of work to do, and boil the potatoes. So a lot of people need to do a lot of things to make the soup tasty. I was more aware of all the steps to make the soup.
—**ROMI**, age 11

Over the years I've had many parents share with me that their child has taught them mindfulness and encouraged them to breathe during stressful situations or practice gratitude when they are feeling down. When we practice, share, and model mindfulness it touches the lives of not only your students but their families and communities. As a teacher you never know how many lives you will influence—your teaching continues on.

CHAPTER SIX

EVERYDAY ACTIVITIES

I put on my shoes with awareness every time. I felt good that I finally thought about how lucky I am to even have shoes. I never thought about that before! Now whenever I put on my shoes I feel how lucky I am.
—KATJA, age 10

WE CAN BRING mindfulness into everything we do. To start, it would be good to focus on taking a few activities you do daily and commit to doing them mindfully. For example, you could use your bathroom time to practice mindfulness while brushing your teeth, showering, and even using the toilet. During a busy school day, sometimes the only private break I get is when I'm in the bathroom. I always use this time to breathe and come back to my body.

My husband and I occasionally attend a San Francisco meditation group called Dharma Punx. These Friday night meditations usually involve entertaining and irreverent spiritual talks, but the main appeal is in their accessibility—every talk relates mindfulness to our lives in a very real way. I remember one talk where the teacher shared that some of his best meditations happened while going to the bathroom. Well, depending on how long your trips to the bathroom last, you may spend between one and a half to four years on the toilet. We all have to use the bathroom. Relieving ourselves instantly brings us back into our bodies—what better time to practice mindfulness?

Driving is also a great opportunity to practice mindfulness. Have you ever gotten in your car and—all of a sudden—you're at your destination and can't recall much of your drive? You were on autopilot the entire time. Bringing awareness to your breathing as you drive is a great way to practice mindfulness effortlessly.

If you play a sport or have another activity that you do regularly, those windows of time can also become opportunities to enjoy mindfulness. Swimming, for me, has become a great time to practice. I already have to focus on my breath, and expanding my awareness to how my body feels gliding through the water is a wonderful way to come back to myself and be fully present in the moment.

Awareness of breath and body during everyday activities is an easy way to access the present moment and bolster your informal mindfulness practice. Choose one activity you engage in every day and try to consistently bring mindfulness to that activity—tying your shoes, cooking, combing your hair, and so on.

THE THREE TS

When I run workshops with Indian teachers, I usually give them my "Three Ts," which are Tea time, Transitional time, and Toilet time. I invite teachers to engage in mindful breathing and mindful drinking whenever they drink tea, since taking a chai break in India is a part of their everyday routine. I also taught them the gatha for drinking tea, "This cup of tea in my two hands, mindfulness held perfectly. My mind and body dwell in the very here and now. In the United States, we could say the same for each coffee break or visit to the water cooler. Transitional time refers to all the time we spend waiting, in line, in traffic, and so on. Apparently, if we live to be seventy years old, we will spend three years of our life waiting.[7] Imagine if we spent all that time practicing mindfulness instead of feeling annoyed and stressed that we have to wait! Whenever I'm waiting in a line, I remind myself that I can choose to spend this time nourishing myself by breathing mindfully, becoming aware of my body, and letting go of tension.

On a busy day, time on the toilet may be the only break you get. I have little reminders placed everywhere in my bathroom to remind me to enjoy the time. Here are a few suggestions from Thich Nhat Hanh's *Present Moment, Wonderful Moment*:

> **Turning on the Water:** Water comes from high mountain sources. Water runs deep in the Earth. Miraculously, water comes to us and sustains all life. My gratitude is filled to the brim.
>
> **Washing Your Hands:** Water flows over these hands. May I use them skillfully to preserve our precious planet.
>
> **Brushing Your Teeth:** Brushing my teeth and rinsing my mouth, I vow to speak purely and lovingly. When my mouth is fragrant with right speech, a flower blooms in the garden of my heart.
>
> **Looking in the Mirror:** Awareness is a mirror reflecting the four elements. Beauty is a heart that generates love and a mind that is open.
>
> **Using the Toilet:** Defiled or immaculate, increasing or decreasing—these concepts exist only in our mind. The reality of interbeing is unsurpassed.

CHAPTER SEVEN

WATERING HELPFUL SEEDS

Our helpful seeds are the positive things about us, which means things that make us good and happy. If we water our helpful seeds, we can pass them on and make other people happy. I think mindfulness means a lot to me because if I don't get my helpful seeds watered, I will get my unhelpful seeds watered, and by doing that, I'm showing that I am not so positive. Without our helpful seeds we are not happy. We all need happiness. **—SEB, age 10**

WE ALL HAVE helpful and unhelpful seeds of emotion inside of us. Depending on what seeds we choose to water, certain seeds grow more than others. Mindfulness helps us build awareness around what seeds we are watering. For example, when I tell my students that I care about them, and I act in caring ways, I water helpful seeds inside of them and inside myself. When I practice deep relaxation or mindful breathing, I water seeds of peace inside myself. When I don't work with challenging emotions and instead react by yelling or engaging in hurtful or destructive behavior, I water unhelpful seeds. The more I water certain seeds, the stronger they grow. My husband and I have committed to a practice of "selective watering" in which we try our best to water only the helpful seeds in each other. When I share this practice with my students we also commit to watering helpful seeds in each other so we can partner in becoming the best we can be.

I've learned that the most important practice of all is to water helpful seeds in *myself.* I find using strategies like BCOOL—that my friend Sister Chau Nghiem (Sr. Jewel), a nun in the Plum Village community, came up with to work with challenging emotions—very effective in helping me water my own helpful seeds. BCOOL stands for:

> **B**reathe,
> **C**alm yourself down,
> know that the situation is **O**kay,
> **O**bserve what's happening inside,
> and hold it with **L**ove.

First, when you notice a strong emotion, take some deep **BREATHS** so you can then **CALM** yourself down. Once you calm yourself down you'll know that you are ultimately **OKAY** and that whatever you are facing is workable. We need to be able to accept whatever we are experiencing. Once you feel better you can **OBSERVE** what's happening inside you, name the emotions, and look deeply into why those emotions are there. As you do this make sure to send yourself **LOVE**: this is the practice of self-compassion that is so critical when working with strong emotions.

A visual I use often when I'm experiencing strong emotions is that of a tree caught in a storm—the branches and leaves may be thrashing and crashing around the tree but the trunk remains rooted; mindfulness helps me stay rooted in my breathing even when I'm experiencing strong emotions. When I breathe through these strong emotions, I calm the leaves and branches down.

Sister Chau Nghiem also taught me the importance of nurturing our helpful, positive mental states to strengthen those seeds. She encouraged me to write a letter, sing, or journal when I'm feeling exceptionally joyful; this helps me keep alive that positive mental state and fortify that seed.

When I initially began teaching my students about seed watering I used the terms "good" and "bad," but thankfully, soon after I began, my friend Myla Kabat-Zinn looked through my lesson plans and in her feedback she shared the importance of using the language of "helpful" and "unhelpful" seeds instead. Good and bad implies judgment, and mindfulness is not about judging. It does call for discernment: you recognize when you've been unskillful, but instead of berating yourself you also look deeply into the causes of your unskillfulness so you can behave in a more thoughtful way in the future. Remember to be kind and gentle to yourself. Of course, younger children may still use the words "good" and "bad."

Learning a little bit about how my brain reacts to stress has also been helpful in working with strong emotions. If I'm stressed out, fearful, or filled with anger my amygdala reacts, bypassing my conscious awareness, resulting in a "fight, flight, or freeze," response. However, if I can learn to stop and breathe when I recognize I'm experiencing a strong emotion, I'll be able to access my prefrontal cortex, the part of my brain that can make thoughtful decisions. When I share this with students I use a clear plastic bottle that I fill with water and glitter, and then shake it to represent an experience of a strong emotion or high stress when our amygdala is reacting. Then, once the shaking stops we breathe mindfully as the glitter settles down to the bottom representing that as we settle down we are able to make better decisions.

Mindfulness is empowering because it helps us see that in every moment we have a choice; we can choose to be more skillful, and there are strategies to support us in watering helpful seeds.

> Don't dwell on the past or the future. Stay with the present and be aware of things around you. And you should water helpful seeds, not unhelpful ones.
>
> —**ARYAN,** age 10

"Mindfulness is being calm, fair, open-minded. To me it means being patient toward other people and taking on a lot of responsibility and caring for them. It is important to water our helpful seeds and the helpful seeds of others because then everyone would be kind and helpful and also to understand other people's feelings. The people who water their helpful seeds will water the helpful seeds of others."

—**EMILY**, age 11

"Mindfulness is kinda like medicine for your brain. And if you're brain is all sick or it's angry you can do mindfulness and it's like, it's medicine."

—**OLIVER**, age 11

"Last year when there was something I didn't know, I would pretend to get a drink of water or go to the bathroom to try to not answer it. But I think mindfulness has made me more confident—instead of just backing away it's helped me face down those fears and that's been really helpful."

— **ANNIE,** age 11

PART II

SHARING MINDFULNESS

CHAPTER EIGHT

LEADING WITH LOVE

Looking at people and communicating that they can be loved, and that they can love in return, is giving them a tremendous gift. It is also a gift to ourselves. We see that we are one with the fabric of life.
—SHARON SALZBERG[8]

BY NOW YOU'VE seen that a peaceful classroom begins with a peaceful you. Mindfulness practice helps me touch a space of peace within myself during the hectic school day. The conscious breaths I now take while drinking in slow sips of tea in my breaks, the mindful steps to my classroom, and even my moments in the bathroom between classes rejuvenate me so I can be awake to the beautiful smiles of my students and meet them with joy and ease. These mindful moments nourish me when I can easily feel just too overwhelmed. Practicing mindfulness has helped me see that even when the waves are very turbulent, I can always dive deep into the ocean of peace I have inside. Now when I'm stressed out or upset I'm able to settle into my breathing, recognize what I feel (which automatically diminishes the intensity of the emotion), and practice acceptance in a nonjudgmental way.

Embracing whatever arises helps me see that I am not my emotion and it brings me a sense of peace. When mindfulness teacher Jon Kabat-Zinn visited my school in India, he instructed me and my colleagues to hold a thought with our awareness. He then asked us what was bigger, the thought or our awareness. This simple exercise was a great reminder that our all-embracing awareness is always larger than our thoughts or what we are feeling. After this exercise, I began calling my mindfulness practice "the ultimate embrace." The ultimate embrace of holding and labeling my strong emotions, thoughts, and sensations as pleasant, unpleasant, or neutral helps me identify with them less as "being me" and more as just what I am experiencing now in the moment. By loosening my identification with my experiences, I'm able to look more closely at them; this investigation leads to understanding what's happening in the moment, which in turn harvests insight. Thich Nhat Hanh teaches us to soothe our strong emotions through invoking the image of a mother holding her crying baby. Just as the mother embraces her crying child with love, we too can hold our strong emotions with tenderness.

In my role as a middle school academic-support teacher at an international school in India, I provided one-on-one instructional support in a variety of subjects. My students would keep a journal, which we would work in every time we met. One of my students, Eliza, regularly forgot her journal in her humanities teacher's classroom.

When I took Eliza to her teacher's classroom to get her journal, Eliza's brilliant, talented teacher yelled, "Oh, this is really stressing me out! How could she forget her journal?" My colleague was without enough strategies to cope with all of the demands placed on her during the school day, so even the smallest thing going wrong became a source of stress.

When we returned to my own classroom, I explained to Eliza that her teacher really cares about her and tried to communicate how much pressure she was under. Then, after school I stopped by my colleague's classroom to check in and ask if she was available for ten minutes to chat about the student we both served. When we sat down I first acknowledged what an amazing job she was doing and sympathized with all the demands she had had placed on her. Then

I asked what I could do to better support her and partner with her as we worked with Eliza. My colleague detailed how much it bothered her when Eliza forgot her journal. When I asked her why, she explained that she was worried that Eliza would fall behind because she didn't have the materials she needed in class. "So you have deep concern for Eliza and care that she succeeds?" I asked.

"Yes! I want her to be successful in my class and I'm frustrated when she forgets the materials she needs to do the work."

"Well, I think if you share that with Eliza, it may make a difference in her remembering her materials. For example, 'Eliza, I really care about you. When you forget your journal, I get stressed because I want you to succeed and I'm concerned that you'll fall behind when you don't have the materials you need.'"

"Do you really think it would make a difference?" my colleague asked.

"Eliza is a pretty sensitive girl and just knowing what you've shared with me now, how much you care about her, could make a huge difference."

The next day when Eliza came to my class she was smiling and she had her journal. "Ms. Meena! I have my journal and Ms. Z was really nice to me today. She just wants to make sure I do well."

The most powerful way we teach is through our actions. How we handle whatever comes our way in the classroom is a model for our students. I've found that meeting challenging situations and students with love and understanding takes tremendous patience and a regular mindfulness practice.

When I was growing up, peace was always an abstract concept. It wasn't until I practiced mindfulness that peace became a little more tangible. Peace is a choice we make in each moment and all we can do as educators is to plant seeds of awareness and peace. We don't know if they will ever bloom. Once you begin practicing mindfulness, you will see how it begins to infuse your day.

LOVING KINDNESS

For me, teaching is driven entirely by love. Leading with love is revolutionary, but it was certainly not something talked about in any of my academic preparation to become a teacher. Yet, without love we feel disconnected and alone, and this causes so much suffering. Love is essential to the classroom.

During my morning mindfulness time before I leave for school or in my classroom before students arrive, I send myself loving kindness. I do this by first bringing awareness to my breathing and calming my body. I then visualize a warm, glowing light in my heart and connect with an image of myself in my mind's eye hugging myself, while saying silently with each breath "You are loved" at least five times. When students enter the classroom I try to make eye contact with each one of them and send them loving kindness energy from my heart: "Grace, you are loved. Jacob, you are loved. Ruby, you are loved." This may sound dubious, but in fact this practice helps me get into a warm, loving state before I greet my students and it does wonders to really humanize and harmonize my relationship with them. I try to radiate love from my heart when I teach, especially when I have a student that's going through a tough time, whether it's their parents' divorce, a sick parent, or a lost soccer match. If you think back to your own childhood and try to remember your own school experiences, you might see that this warm bond of loving kindness was present between yourself and the teachers you liked best, even if they didn't practice mindfulness as a learned skill.

I've also expanded the practice to my colleagues and the parents of my students. I remind myself that we all just wish to feel happy and loved and through sending loving kindness I'm able to lessen this sense of being separate. We are all partners in this work of touching the hearts and minds of our young people.

I send love to my cousin who is nine. His mother just died so I'm sending him love so he'll stop being sad.
—**ANANT,** age 11

I send love to my mom so she becomes healthy. I send love to my grandpa because he misses me. I sent love to my stepmom because her mom died on Friday.
—**THEODORE,** age 10

I sent my uncle who is in the hospital love and caring because he is suffering from a liver problem.
—**NIKHIL,** age 11

I sent happiness and love to my grandma since she tried so hard to make people happy and she is so nice to everyone and I don't really do anything for her . . . so yeah.
—**JAIVEER,** age 11

I wish everyone in the world be happy regardless of how rich or poor they are. I wish everyone will be peaceful and there will not be war. I wish that everyone will be kind to each other.
—**SEE KAI,** age 10

We relaxed and closed our eyes and focused on our breathing. Ms. Srinivasan told us that our best friend is our breath because that is what leaves us last, and that we should listen to it very closely. We were then asked to choose someone who is having a hard time with life at the moment and to send our blessings to them. This was very hard as I see so many people that I know having a rough time right now, but in the end I chose my grandmother and tried to send out positive thoughts and prayers for her general well-being. After our blessings, we focused on Delhi, the whole of India, then Asia, and finally the whole earth. Mindfulness is very calming and I personally have the feeling of sleeping but being awake at the same time. I felt like I was alone and at peace with myself. This practice allowed some time to get in touch with our true selves.

—**NINA,** age 14

CHAPTER NINE

SEEING OTHERS AS YOURSELF

We are caught in an inescapable network of mutuality, tied in a single garment of destiny. Whatever affects one directly, affects all indirectly.
—MARTIN LUTHER KING, JR.

WHEN SHARING MINDFULNESS with your students it's crucial to understand that all you are doing is planting seeds; you don't know if, how, or when they will bloom. I say this because so often we can become frustrated that we don't see the immediate results of sharing the practice. I've had experiences when I'm not sure if I am really reaching a student and months or even years later I receive a letter from that very same student divulging that mindfulness has helped them tremendously and is now a large part of their life.

Breathing in, I listen to my students.
Breathing out, I hear what they say.

When I share mindfulness with my students, I always frame it as an invitation and never impose mindful practice on any of them. Rather, I ask them to be open to what I have to offer, and if they don't connect with it, that's fine. It's important for students to feel safe and comfortable, and if they view it as an opportunity instead of a requirement, their participation will be more genuine. Through modeling the practice myself, my students see how I integrate mindfulness into my life. For example, sometimes I may share with students that I really need to invite the bell and practice mindful breathing so I can truly be present for them. A few years ago, my students tell me, they had a teacher who always talked about "mindful listening"—but she never listened to her students! When she tried to share practices that she didn't embody or have real experience with the students responded unfavorably.

Educator Parker Palmer often talks about how teachers teach who we are; the most important way we share mindfulness is through our authentic presence. We can't teach peace or happiness; we must *be* peace and happiness and transmit our state, our way of being, to our students.

Relationships are fundamental to teaching. I've learned that sharing mindfulness in the classroom has the potential to develop powerful connections with students. Four years ago, I received a very unexpected email from a student, Trina, that brought tears to my eyes. Trina had sent me a message with a recording of her voice talking about mindfulness—completely unprompted. While I've gotten touching cards from students during my decade as an educator, I've never received anything so directly tied to how bringing the practice of mindfulness into the classroom can affect a student's life for the better. Just weeks before I received Trina's email I was kicking myself because only a few of my sixth graders seemed to understand the importance of acceptance when practicing mindfulness.

While I was living in India I had the honor and privilege of organizing multiple visits of His Holiness the Karmapa, the second most important Tibetan spiritual leader after the Dalai Lama, to my school in Delhi. When I asked him for some guidance on teaching mindfulness to my students, he told me that children are able to access mindfulness much easier than adults. Our adult minds are full of thinking and years of conditioning that feed unhelpful emotions; in contrast, some of our younger students have relatively few years of negative conditioning. In teaching mindfulness, what matters most is opening our hearts, loving and connecting with our students, and trusting they will get what they need or what they are supposed to have received.

Trina sent me this record of her thoughts on mindfulness:

> Mindfulness to me means to calm yourself, to look and observe yourself and see how you react. Mindfulness leads to a better person, the person is inside you. It is a way to express your insight, to make it come alive, to make yourself a better person, to make yourself more calmer and a time to correct your mistakes. Mindfulness is really something really, really, really strong and it helps you in many ways. And really mindfulness is not just about being calm it can change so many of your habits. It can change most of your habits and it really helps you be present, be alive in this moment. Mindfulness is about making yourself a better person to love yourself and making yourself a better human being to everybody. Mindfulness helps me.

Trina didn't receive grades for my class, and while it is true that students act in ways to please their teachers, I do believe Trina was touched by mindfulness in a very special way. In W. H. Auden's *The Old School*, the author writes, "For a teacher to be of real value to his pupils, he must above all be a happy person."[9] It's not always about what you teach but how you teach it, and the love and joy behind your teaching is perhaps the strongest impression you will leave with your students.

A few years later, I had a student who I was sure I wasn't connecting with at all. Then, on the last day of school she handed me this:

Dear Meena,

I just wanted to say how great it has been having you as a teacher. There have been many teachers who have changed the way I learn but you're the only one who has also changed me as a person and who I am. Every time I count my blessings I count you.

Love, Grace

Mindfulness taught without love would not have affected these students in the same way. That being said, it's important to monitor ourselves as we teach mindfulness. Our students may admire us for infusing our teaching of mindfulness with love but this is really just a reflection of all the beauty that lies within each of us.

Some students are not going to immediately connect to mindfulness, just as some may not instantly connect to algebra. When I have a student that doesn't connect to what I'm teaching, regardless of subject, I do my best to find out what the student is interested in or passionate about. Then I find innovative ways to connect my lessons to their interests. For example, I had a star basketball player, Jaime, roll his eyes throughout my first mindfulness class. I found him during lunch that same day, acknowledged that I noticed he didn't seem to be engaged with the mindfulness material and that I was fine with that, but I wasn't okay with him rolling his eyes because I felt hurt and disrespected. I then asked him why he didn't connect to what I was teaching, and he shared that mindfulness doesn't relate to anything he cares about—he was bored. We made a deal: I committed to making mindfulness more relevant to what he cares about, and Jaime committed to being respectful and more open to what I was teaching. Before our next class, I researched everything I could that connected mindfulness to basketball. I learned about how Phil Jackson, the former NBA coach of the Los Angeles Lakers and Chicago Bulls, used mindfulness to create winning teams. In our next class, when I shared video clips and quotes connecting mindfulness and basketball, Jaime was completely engaged and he participated beautifully in my class throughout the semester. The following year he would occasionally stop by my classroom to invite the bell and practice mindful breathing. In order for Jaime to be open to mindfulness he had to know that I cared enough to make mindfulness matter to him.

EMPATHY

Empathy involves understanding another person from his or her perspective. You put yourself in others' shoes to try and experience what they are feeling. Seeing students, colleagues, and parents as yourself increases compassion, altruism, and prosocial behavior—essential qualities for a thriving school community.

In preparation for classes, faculty meetings, and parent conferences, I try to see myself as my students, my colleagues, or the parents of my students. Before connecting with people, this practice helps me gain perspective and go into my class, meeting, or conference with much more ease. For example, when my students act up I try to remember what I was like as an adolescent and in doing this I'm able to approach the situation in a much more authentic, lighthearted way.

A few years ago I was charged with teaching sixth-grade health, which focused on puberty. Connecting with my inner sixth grader, I anticipated giggles when we began using the words "penis" and "vagina," so I had my entire class scream each word out loud five times. The first few times the screams were followed by uproarious laughter but eventually the students got the hilariousness of it all out of their system and we could move forward with the lesson.

Similarly, when we engage in mindful breathing, if suddenly amidst the calm and quiet there's the sound of a fart, I don't pretend that nothing happened. If I were in sixth grade and a classmate farted while we were mindfully breathing, I would have giggled too! Since no one student in particular should be singled out as the farter, I simply acknowledge that "gas has passed," say, "this is a natural bodily function," and allow my students to settle down.

Since I'm not yet a parent, it can be a little more of a reach to put myself in my students' parents' shoes, but before each parent conference it helps me to first bring awareness to my breathing for a minute or two and silently say to myself, "Breathing in, I see myself as the parent of ______________ (child's name). Breathing out, I recognize we are a team and we want the best for ______________ (child's name)."

With certain parents who I know are open to practicing mindfulness, we've invited the bell together before the conference began and have spent time breathing for a minute to connect to how we are both a team and are at this conference to support their child's academic and social-emotional well-being.

It's easiest for me to see myself as my colleagues because I understand the professional demands placed on them to perform in the classroom. Acknowledging these demands and any other challenges I may know they are facing outside of the classroom (sick parent, challenging partner, weight loss) helps broaden my perspective so I can better relate and connect to them in meetings.

LOVE LETTERS AND GRADING

My most recent teaching assignment was at a school where we didn't have letter grades; as an alternative to report cards, teachers at this school wrote lengthy narratives about each child. Instead of dreading the several weekends I spent writing these reports each semester, I tried to look at it as an opportunity to send loving kindness to my students. The process of writing these "love letter" reports became truly enjoyable. I was honest in my assessment of each student and reflected on areas that needed strengthening, but the process also made me look deeply at each child, recognize their gifts, and highlight their uniqueness in the reports.

CHAPTER TEN

THE STRATEGIES YOU ALREADY HAVE

AFTER A DECADE as a classroom teacher, I transitioned out of the classroom and now work in the social emotional learning and leadership development department of a large urban public school district, where I strive to enhance the instructional capacity of leaders and teachers in social emotional learning. Through this work I've learned the importance of having educators examine the strategies they may already have around mindfulness. When contemplating your personal and classroom practice, think about opportunities you're given to cultivate a deeper awareness, periods of time dedicated for reflection, or strategies you employ when you face a difficulty.

At my school in India, in honor of the UN International Day of Peace we had all of our middle school students reflect on their feelings in an attempt to gain greater awareness of what peace is. For one week they recorded their feelings and when, where, and why they experienced them in a "Peace Log." Students were then asked to come up with strategies to help transform their nonpeaceful thoughts, speech, and actions. Through this activity, students and colleagues were able to spend some time reflecting on what strategies they already had to work with challenging thoughts, situations, and emotions.

Taking some time now to detail what strategies you already employ is a great idea; you may discover that you are already practicing aspects of mindfulness!

STUDENT REFLECTIONS FROM THEIR PEACE LOGS

"Breathing: It makes me calm and gave me time to understand the situation."

"Understanding why we are feeling the way we feel: It helps me understand the situation."

"Spending time with nature and people we love: It made me cheerful and joyful."

"Thinking about what we are grateful for: I feel lucky and blessed."

"Seeking to understand the bigger picture: It helped me understand what was going on."

"Smiling: Makes everyone happy."

"Helping others: Takes my worries away."

"Helping others: Understanding other people's problems. Thinking deeply of how to help others."

CHAPTER ELEVEN

GRATITUDE AND INTERBEING

Mindfulness means to be aware of what you are doing and being grateful for what you have.
—**WILLIAM, age 12**

FOCUSING ON WHAT I'm grateful for is one of the quickest ways to shift my mood and feel good. According to the research of Professor Bob Emmons at the University of California, Davis, a regular gratitude practice can increase your happiness by 25 percent![10] So what is a regular gratitude practice? It involves more than just naming and noticing the things you are grateful for every now and then. A regular gratitude practice must involve writing down what you are grateful for with feeling. If possible, try and make it part of your daily routine and set aside time in the morning or evening. One year I had my students create gratitude journals and I kept one along with them and every day we would take time to reflect on what we are grateful for. My husband, Chihiro, and I now keep a gratitude journal. Regularly taking time to reflect on what we are grateful for waters the helpful seeds in our relationship.

Just as routines and rituals are essential for the classroom, I suggest creating a daily ritual to take five to ten minutes every evening for gratitude practice. My husband learned the following gratitude practice from Linda Graham, a mindfulness teacher who spoke in a course he took on cultivating joy. First write down with feeling everything you are grateful for that is a noun. Be specific: Instead of "loved ones," name your loved ones. Try to invoke the image of each item you name; if you write down "home," visualize your home. If you write down "parents," visualize your parents. Then, write down all the verbs you are grateful for. As you write, visualize yourself engaging in these actions: see yourself sleeping soundly, eating a delicious meal, listening to your favorite music, and so on. Finally, write down whatever you feel is connected to your web of life—take note of who or what are you connected with, such as the farmers who grow the apples you love, the sanitation workers who keep your city clean, the cashier at the supermarket who bagged your groceries. Enlist a friend or family member to be your gratitude buddy. You can share your gratitude list with them daily via email or phone, or in person if it's someone you live with. Sharing gratitude is infectious; it waters seeds of joy inside ourselves and in others.

My former colleague, Pam Nicholls, a rock-star learning specialist, introduced me to the practice of HeartMath a few years ago. HeartMath technology helps us measure our heart-rate variability so we can use our heart rhythms to better manage our emotions. Pam and I even cotaught HeartMath to my students and would practice together during our lunch breaks. In addition to mindful breathing techniques, HeartMath focuses on sustaining positive emotions. Through HeartMath I learned that breathing through my heart while simultaneously focusing on feelings of appreciation and gratitude decreased stress and increased my energy levels. As a result, when I engaged in gratitude or appreciation practice with my students, I encouraged them to practice heart-centered breathing.

We can only be said to be alive in those moments when our hearts are conscious of our treasures. —**THORNTON WILDER**

The practice of gratitude helps me see that my existence is dependent on so much that is freely and generously given—from the five elements of nature to the love I receive from my family. Even when I'm having a very challenging day I can still find something to be grateful for, and this automatically puts me in a more generous, kind, and loving frame of mind.

The concept of interbeing means that nothing exists independently. When we practice gratitude, we can recognize this at a deep level in our lives. Interbeing is best expressed in Thich Nhat Hanh's writings:

> If you are a poet, you will see clearly that there is a cloud floating in this sheet of paper. Without a cloud, there will be no rain; without rain, the trees cannot grow; and without trees, we cannot make paper. The cloud is essential for the paper to exist. If the cloud is not here, the sheet of paper cannot be here either. So we can say that the cloud and the paper inter-are. "Interbeing" is a word that is not in the dictionary yet, but if we combine the prefix "inter-" with the verb "to be," we have a new verb, inter-be.[11]

I often share this with my students before we practice mindful eating. Over the years I've found it very helpful to use the concept of interbeing when working with teachers and colleagues to help us see that our school can only work with all of its multiple parts working smoothly. If one part of the system functions poorly, the whole body of the school is affected. Sometimes there can be challenges between different entities within schools, but if we can remember that without the administration, parents, staff, and students, our schools would not be able to function, we can approach our interactions with others in our community with more gratitude and understanding.

CHAPTER TWELVE

STARTING A MINDFUL PRACTICE GROUP

A GREAT WAY to support your practice is to start a mindful practice group at your school. You could meet once a week either before or after school, or if that's too much, start with meeting once or twice a month. Perhaps you can use your classroom or talk with an administrator about using a common space to meet. Even though this space should be confidential so all participants feel safe expressing themselves, I suggest forming various practice groups to suit people's needs. For example, there could be a group for the entire school community or one just for teachers or just for parents. I had an experience where some of my teaching colleagues felt that if there were administrators or parents in the group, they would not feel comfortable or safe that the group would honor how they truly felt. So it's important to create safe spaces in which individuals feel they can express themselves without being afraid of being criticized later.

A mindful practice group can also include educators in your area and be as small as you and another person! The purpose of such groups is to nurture growth, support each other, witness mindfulness practice lived out, and contribute to sustainability. Some benefits of starting a group at your school include building on common ground, serving as "mindfulness bells" for each other during the school day, and cultivating mindfulness in your community. Some ideas for generating interest in the practice group include making student learning about mindfulness visible through sharing at a faculty meeting or school publication, hosting a half day of mindfulness in which you lead colleagues through some of the practices outlined in this guide, or starting a faculty book club where you read and discuss books with a mindful education focus.

When forming a community of practice, there are some things you'll want to keep in mind. First you need to assess the skills and interest level of those who want to participate. As in any group or club, you then need to define roles, such as who will be responsible for hosting and snacks, who will coordinate communication with those interested, who will lead the practices (or if you will rotate), and so on. It is important to develop a leadership model and choose if there will be one leader or shared leadership. Decide what your meeting structure will be like, including how often you will meet and the practices your group wants to explore.

When you decide on a space to hold your mindful practice group, take some time to make the space feel inviting. Even if it's in a classroom after school, taking the time to arrange chairs in a circle and place a flower in the middle or light a candle can transform the space. When my Social Emotional Learning team conducts Professional Learning we always use colorful tablecloths. Colorful tablecloths can transform a dingy gym or auditorium and they send the message that you care.

When your group meets for the first time it would be a good idea to spend some time creating agreements or norms that guide your time together. The Center for Courage and Renewal (www.couragerenewal.org) uses inspiring touchstones to guide their Circle of Trust groups. My favorite is "Believe that it's possible to emerge refreshed, surprised, and less burdened than when we came."[12]

A mindful practice group can explore ways of practicing, learn together through reading and listening to mindfulness teachings, and connect with the greater community through "mindfulness field trips" to hear talks, practice in alternative settings, and attend workshops. Most of all, participating in the group should be enjoyable and nourishing for the soul. Teachers are so busy they have little room for adding activities that are not truly enhancing to their professional development or their personal lives.

My friend and former colleague Adele Caemmerer came up with a practice group "menu" that I often draw from.

PRACTICE GROUP MENU

> Listen, listen, this wonderful sound brings me back to my true self.
>
> —THICH NHAT HANH

Once participants have gathered and gotten comfortable, I usually invite the bell. I do this because it engages our sense of hearing and it gathers the group and focuses attention. It provides structure and indicates transitions in a nonverbal way. Most importantly, listening to the bell becomes a way of connecting to our inner selves.

Opening (5 minutes)

When everyone has settled in and connected to their breathing, we transition to formally opening the group with three or more sounds of the bell and some brief words that help call the group together and set the intention for the gathering. These words could be a gatha, a poem, or even a song.

Bodywork/Breathing (15 minutes)

For this section I would encourage you to use a collection of breathing meditations in *Blooming of a Lotus* or *Present Moment, Wonderful Moment* by Thich Nhat Hanh, or create your own.[13] The use of the bell deepens experience and gently reminds us to come back to ourselves when our minds wander. Two of my favorites: "In, out, deep, slow; calm, ease, smile, release" or "Breathing in, I see myself as a flower. Breathing out, I feel fresh."

Mindful Movements/Stretching

Have everyone share one stretch or choose ten ahead of time to share with the group. *Mindful Movements: Ten Exercises for Well-Being* by Thich Nhat Hanh is a great resource for this.[14]

Deep Relaxation

You can guide the group through this practice or play a deep relaxation, *yoga nidra*, or body-scan audio recording. Some recommendations for recordings I have used are listed in the Recommended Resources section of this book.

Readings and Practice (20 minutes)

Readings

You can have members rotate to volunteer to bring a reading that has inspired them to share with the group. You can also share excerpts from a book or blog that has inspired your practice. The key when looking for readings is to look for something that will touch, move, and inspire members of your group. Short readings provide focus and a theme for reflection.

Mindful Breathing

Have the group sit for twenty minutes of mindful breathing.

Mindful Walking

If you are near a space that's conducive to walking, have everyone take time to walk mindfully.

Tea, Eating, Object Meditation

Mindfully drinking tea, eating an orange, looking deeply at nature, or engaging in artwork can be wonderfully nourishing activities. Savoring a cup of tea or an orange after a long school day provides opportunities to experience interbeing. Reflecting on nature can help us see how interwoven our lives are. Taking time to draw or paint places us directly in the moment.

Circle Sharing (15 minutes)

This is time where group members can share what's happening for them in their practice. It would be a good idea to come up with guidelines with the group for how you would like to conduct circle sharing. In my experience it can be guided with a suggested theme or can be completely open. Each person who shares speaks from their own experience and process. It's not a discussion and there is no "cross talk" so whoever is speaking can share without interruption. Most importantly, everything shared in the circle is confidential.

Closing (5 minutes)

The closing provides closure and transition to everyday life. It helps members absorb the experience and reflect on their intention. It can take any form that works for your group, whether it be a song, reciting a poem, silence, or reciting a traditional loving-kindness prayer first to yourself and then to all beings. One that my husband and I say at the end of our daily sitting practice is:

May I be happy
May I be healthy
May I live with ease and well-being
May I be safe from inner and outer harm
May I be free from suffering
May I always feel embraced by love

May all beings be well
May all beings be happy
May all beings be healthy
May all beings live with ease and well-being
May all beings be safe from inner and outer harm
May all beings be free from suffering
May all beings always feel embraced by love
—Adapted from Insight Meditation Society

MINDFUL CONSULTANCY

Once there is a sense of trust among each other in your educator mindful practice group you can engage in a Mindful Consultancy to help each other work through any challenges you may be facing both in and out of the classroom. A Mindful Consultancy is a structured way for helping colleagues think more expansively about a dilemma they are experiencing in their work. It is adapted from the Consultancy Protocol, which was developed by Gene Thompson and the National School Reform Faculty, Harmony Education Center. By infusing the Consultancy Protocol with mindful breathing we are more inclined to be fully present as our colleagues share and offer their best guidance in helping us work through our challenges.

Mindful Consultancy Protocol[15]

Time: Sixteen minutes per participant. Select a timekeeper and the order of presentations.

1. **(1 minute)** Practice mindful breathing with your partner(s). It may be helpful to focus on the following gatha during the one-minute breathing periods:

> *Breathing in, I listen to my colleague.*
> *Breathing out, I hear what he/she says.*

2. **(2 minutes)** The presenter gives an overview of the dilemma/question/reflection. This is also a time for the presenter to offer some context.

3. **(1 minute)** Practice mindful breathing with your partner(s).

4. **(3 minutes)** The reflectors ask the presenter clarifying questions. Clarifying questions are for the person asking them. They ask the presenter "Who, What, Where, When, and How." They are not "Why" questions. The clarifying questions can be answered quickly and succinctly, often with just a phrase or two.

5. **(1 minute)** Practice mindful breathing with your partner(s).

6. **(5 minutes)** The reflectors talk with each other (not to the presenter) about the dilemma/questions presented. What did we hear? What didn't we hear that we think might be relevant? What do we think about the dilemma/question? What options might be possible? The presenter does not speak during this discussion, but instead mindfully listens.

7. **(1 minute)** Practice mindful breathing with your partner(s).

8. **(2 minutes)** The presenter responds to the discussion, sharing with the group anything that particularly resonated for him/her. The point of this time period is not for the presenter to give a "blow by blow" response to the group's conversation, nor is it to defend or further explain. Rather, this is a time for the presenter to talk about the most significant comments, ideas, and questions heard. The presenter can also share any new thoughts or questions that emerged while listening to the reflectors.

Make sure you and your partner(s) take time to debrief how the mindful consultancy process was for you. Together you can decide if you want to adapt the protocol to better serve your practice group needs. It would also be useful during this time to draw upon how you used mindfulness during the protocol both formally and informally. You can also reflect on how mindfulness may help you with your dilemma. By doing this you name exactly how you are practicing mindfulness, making it more explicit in your life. I find the mindful consultancy practice incredibly helpful and a great way to get structured support from colleagues. There is so much wisdom and insight all around us, it's important to have structured ways to receive it!

"Mindfulness for me means when you act in the right thoughtful way. When you are aware of all the things that you do. And you have to be cool with yourself and be calm. When you are angry you have to understand why you are angry."

—**ROMI,** age 11

"Mindfulness is controlling your temper and trying to understand other people's situations and difficulties. Mindfulness is also being able to forgive others despite their mistakes. If everyone tries to water each other's helpful seeds and be nice to others, the world would be very peaceful and people would be able to coexist without any wars."

—**JANICE,** age 11

"Mindfulness is thinking before reacting. Mindfulness means something to me because it reduces stress. Watering helpful seeds is important because it makes life easier for us and the people around us."

—**VALENTIN,** age 10

PART III

MINDFULNESS AS A LEARNED SKILL:

A CURRICULUM FOR MINDFUL EDUCATORS

CHAPTER THIRTEEN

MINDFULNESS LESSONS

AFTER SEEING THE positive impact mindfulness practice has had on my life and the lives of my students, and after learning about the research behind the beneficial effects of mind training, I created a mindfulness unit tied to the United States National Health Education Standards, though easily adaptable as standards change. What follows are adaptations of the lessons I used with my students. In developing these lessons I've utilized the Understanding by Design (UbD) curriculum framework, identifying classroom learning goals and planning toward that goal, designing "backward" from the desired classroom outcome. The lessons are concrete with an emphasis on mindfulness as a skill we can build in order to manage our lives more effectively. The way I've structured my curriculum is with a unit plan, which guides the entire unit. It's a snapshot of the main learning takeaways. The course has three essential questions:

Why be mindful?
What is mindfulness?
How can I be mindful?

I frame the questions in this order, starting first with "Why be mindful?" to emphasize the importance of connecting mindfulness to the lives of your students in your introduction and throughout your teaching of mindfulness. Naturally when you start teaching, you have to help students understand **what** mindfulness is before they can understand why it may be helpful, but focusing on the **why** as you continue your teaching is critical because students need to know why you are teaching mindfulness. In order for mindfulness to matter, it has to be accessible and relevant to the lives of your students.

According to Jay McTighe and Grant Wiggins, the founders of UbD: "Essential questions are open-ended with no single, correct answer. They are meant to stimulate inquiry, further questions and be reexamined over the course of the unit. They are designed to be thought-provoking to students, engaging them in sustained, focused inquiries, culminating in meaningful performances."[16]

With each lesson, as students learn more strategies and mindfulness practices, their ability to answer these questions deepens, and by the end of the unit students gain a solid understanding of mindfulness and how (in a practical sense, skill-wise) this can help them in their lives.

In using the UbD process to design my mindfulness unit, I was forced to think with the end in mind by starting with the "enduring understanding" that I wanted for my students. Enduring understandings have lasting value beyond the content I'm teaching; they are what I want my students to take with them for the rest of their lives. They are the reason why I'm teaching what I teach. Framing my curriculum design in this way, I knew that I wanted each of my students to leave my mindfulness unit understanding that mindfulness can help them manage their lives more effectively. Every lesson I taught then focused on trying to develop that understanding in my students. The essential questions help to elicit this enduring understanding.

The Five Core Competencies of Social Emotional Learning (SEL)[17]

Self-awareness: The ability to accurately recognize one's emotions and thoughts and their influence on behavior. This includes accurately assessing one's strengths and limitations and possessing a well-grounded sense of confidence and optimism.

Self-management: The ability to regulate one's emotions, thoughts, and behaviors effectively in different situations. This includes managing stress, controlling impulses, motivating oneself, and setting and working toward achieving personal and academic goals.

Social awareness: The ability to take the perspective of and empathize with others from diverse backgrounds and cultures, to understand social and ethical norms for behavior, and to recognize family, school, and community resources and supports.

Relationship skills: The ability to establish and maintain healthy and rewarding relationships with diverse individuals and groups. This includes communicating clearly, listening actively, cooperating, resisting inappropriate social pressure, negotiating conflict constructively, and seeking and offering help when needed.

Responsible decision making: The ability to make constructive and respectful choices about personal behavior and social interactions based on consideration of ethical standards, safety concerns, social norms, the realistic evaluation of consequences of various actions, and the well-being of self and others.

What I teach is based on what I've experienced as a practitioner of mindfulness. My hope in sharing these lessons is that they may serve as a resource for teachers interested in bringing mindfulness into their classroom and spur more ideas for teachers already doing this work. These lessons aren't exactly what I do in the classroom, because mindfulness means I am in the moment when I am teaching and don't follow a script—I'm totally there with my students and together we are on a journey of discovery. For example, hugging meditation isn't in my lesson plans, but depending on the feel of the classroom, I may teach it! Also, teachers are, at the core, designers. As a mindful teacher I am constantly adapting and revising curriculum in response to the needs of my students. I encourage you to use these lessons as a springboard for developing your own mindful classroom. While this unit specifically mentions the United States National Health Education Standards, as you adapt these lessons for your own use, I'd urge you to also draw on the Five Social and Emotional Learning Core Competencies from the Collaborative for Academic and Social Emotional Learning (www.casel.org).

In my current work, building capacity around social emotional learning in a large urban public school district, we help teachers and administrators see how social emotional skills create conditions for learning. With the adoption of the Common Core State Standards, many United States schools are faced with a pedagogical shift that requires students to have social emotional skills. One of the core instructional shifts, Academic Discussion, calls upon students to co-construct meaning with each other. Mindfulness practice provides students with strategies for practicing the self-awareness, self-management, social awareness, relationship skills, and responsible decision making needed to engage in Academic Discussion.

These lessons are what I've found to be developmentally appropriate for my sixth graders, each lesson corresponding to an eighty-minute block of time. Any experienced educator can adapt the lessons to the age group and the length of their class. The unit also includes handouts and homework assignments detailed in the appendix, that can be made into a "Mindfulness Journal" where students can record all of their reflections during the unit.

I suggest starting off the school year with the mindfulness curriculum. By doing this, you will foster a classroom community and teach the social emotional learning skills needed to create conditions for learning. Then you can embed mindfulness and social emotional learning into your curriculum. I frequently wove both mindfulness and social emotional learning throughout my social studies classes from questions around ethics to civic engagement. I avoid using the word "integrate" because integrate suggests that mindfulness and social emotional learning are separate from academics when in fact they can be foundational to curricular concepts.

I recommend that you share a unit plan and some of the solid research around social emotional learning and mindfulness with your school administrators before you begin teaching mindfulness to your students. In the Recommended Resources section I list some of the research I used when I approached my administrator about teaching mindfulness. I also wrote a letter to parents informing them about what I would be teaching. In this letter I included my unit plan, cited the research articles in the Recommended Resources section and discussed how brain science framed my teaching of mindfulness. In my discussion of brain science, I shared the research of neuroscientist Dr. Richard Davidson from the Center for Investigating Healthy Minds at the Waisman Center, University of Wisconsin, Madison. The work of the Center is grounded in the cutting edge findings around neuroplasticity, "the discovery that our brains change throughout our lives in response to experience, suggesting that positive changes can be nurtured through mental training (mindfulness)."[18] Mindfulness has the potential to help us consciously repattern our brain toward an improved mental, emotional, and physical state. Parents appreciated receiving the letter and as a result, they would ask their child what mindfulness strategies they learned in school, prompting many of my students to teach their parents the skills in turn! It's been gratifying to watch the miracle of mindfulness spread in this way through my school community.

Before engaging in the lessons, it would be useful to review the following facilitation techniques adapted from the Developmental Studies Center[19]:

- To promote cooperative learning, have students "turn to your partner" or "think, pair, share" so everyone has a chance to speak.
- Ask open-ended questions and avoid asking questions that have a "yes" or "no" response.
- Utilize "wait time" before discussing a question or calling on a student so all students have time to think. (You can use this time to take a few mindful breaths for yourself.)
- Try to maintain a neutral stance instead of using praise. For example, ask students: "Why?" or "Can you explain your thinking?" or say "Thank you," instead of praising them. This maintains a fair and just classroom environment.
- Do not paraphrase student comments. Encourage them to listen to each other, not just you, and, if needed, have other students rephrase what a student may have said.
- Encourage students to respond to each other directly. For example, "What do you want to ask Neesha about her thinking process?"
- Ask questions such as, "What can you add to José's explanation?" to help students build on each other's thinking.
- Create an expectation that students look at and listen to the person speaking.

- Try and have students call on each other when you have discussions. (In lesson 2 when the Talking Piece is introduced, it can help facilitate this.)
- Create sentence starters to help students discuss. Some examples are: My idea builds on ________'s idea because ________. While I can see why you believe this, I see it differently. In my opinion ________. I understand where you are coming from, but I see it a bit differently. From my perspective, ________.

UNIT PLAN
MINDFULNESS AS A LEARNED SKILL

Stage One — Desired Results

SUMMARY

This unit is an exploration and application of mindfulness. Its goal is to provide students with experiential understanding of mindfulness as a skill they can cultivate to manage their lives more effectively. It is the experience of the course instructor that mindfulness is a skill we can cultivate to enhance our ability to:

- Maintain/focus attention
- Work skillfully with our emotions
- Manage stress
- Develop a sense of inner peace
- Promote compassion and kindness towards oneself and others
- Be resilient
- Recognize interdependence/interconnection

- Foster understanding
- Communicate effectively
- Make healthy decisions.

Mindfulness must be the foundation of Social Emotional Learning (SEL) because it teaches students how to cultivate self-awareness, the first of the five SEL Core Competencies. SEL helps students "develop the fundamental skills for life effectiveness. SEL teaches the skills we all need to handle ourselves, our relationships, and our work, effectively and ethically. These skills include recognizing and managing our emotions, developing caring and concern for others, establishing positive relationships, making responsible decisions, and handling challenging situations constructively and ethically. They are the skills that allow children to calm themselves when angry, make friends, resolve conflicts respectfully, and make ethical and safe choices."[20]

UNITED STATES NATIONAL HEALTH EDUCATION

STANDARDS AND BENCHMARKS[21]

Grade 6–8 National Health Education Standard: Students will demonstrate the ability to practice health-enhancing behaviors and avoid or reduce health risks. As a result of health instruction in grades 6–8, we will observe the following benchmarks for students:

- Explain the importance of assuming responsibility for personal health behaviors.
- Demonstrate healthy practices and behaviors that will maintain or improve the health of self and others.

Grade 6–8 National Health Education Standard: Students will demonstrate the ability to use goal-setting skills to enhance health.

The benchmarks are:

- Assess personal health practices.
- Develop a goal to adopt, maintain, or improve a personal health practice.
- Apply strategies and skills needed to attain a personal health goal.

ENDURING UNDERSTANDING

Students will understand: Being mindful can help me manage my life more effectively.

ESSENTIAL QUESTIONS

Why be mindful?
What is mindfulness?
How can I be mindful?

KNOWLEDGE CONTENT

Students know:

- Whenever your mind becomes scattered, you can use your breath to come back to yourself.
- You can use mindfulness to calm yourself, reduce stress, work skillfully with strong emotions, and maintain focus.
- Mindfulness enables us to consciously repattern our brain toward an improved mental, emotional, and physical state.

SKILLS

Students will be able to:

- Recognize when they are not present.
- Keep the mind focused by using the breath as an

anchor.

- Utilize various practices to balance the mind such as moving attention from one body part to another (mindful movements, simple stretches, deep relaxation).
- Send well-being to others.
- Consider the well-being of a loved one.
- Recognize, accept, and then try to understand challenging mental states and strong emotions.
- See how their own behavior and choices affect others.
- See the benefit of thinking and considering outcomes before they act.
- Communicate effectively and listen actively.
- Use their breath to connect their body and mind.

Stage Two — Assessment Evidence

STANDARDS AND BENCHMARKS

Students will assess the way they manage stress, develop a goal, and apply mindfulness-based strategies and keep a journal as they maintain and improve their management of stress. Students explain the importance of taking responsibility for personal health behaviors through class discussions. Students demonstrate healthy practices through participation in class activities and their mindfulness journal. Class discussions guide students to find examples of when they applied their mindfulness practice in real life and explain why they think it helped/didn't help. This connects to both the application of strategies and skills benchmark for the first standard and the demonstration of healthy practices that will maintain or improve health of self and others for the second.

Before you begin teaching mindfulness present your students

with a stressful scenario and have them describe how they'd handle it. Revisit the same scenario at the end of the unit and see if students now approach the stressful situation differently.

RUBRIC FOR ASSESSMENT

Keeping in mind the enduring understanding, "Mindfulness is a skill I can cultivate to help me manage my life more effectively," and the National Health Education Standards outlined on page 97, evaluate students at the end of the unit, taking into account class participation, their answers to how they handle stressful situations, and their mindfulness journals. Instructors are encouraged to write a personal letter to each student explaining why they received the evaluation they did and draw from notes the instructor has taken after each class, student journals, and student answers to how they handle a stressful situation. In addition to reading their students' mindfulness journals after each lesson, it is important for the instructor to reflect on each student during class time at each session to see how they are connecting with the material.

The rubric below can be used by teachers to assess student understanding and application of mindfulness. The rubric can also be adapted for student self-assessment of mindfulness.

	NOT YET	BEGINNING	DEVELOPING	SECURE
	Shows very little understanding of mindfulness. Needs ongoing support.	Shows some understanding of mindfulness. Needs regular support.	Shows understanding of mindfulness. Needs some support.	Consistently understands and applies mindfulness independently.

ENDURING UNDERSTANDING				
Mindfulness is a skill I can cultivate to help me manage my life more effectively.				

Stage Three — Learning Plan

Understanding the importance of modeling mindfulness in order to teach it, before each class the instructor engages in a mindfulness practice as specified in each lesson.

CLASS TOPICS

Lesson 1 Being Present through Breath Awareness
Lesson 2 Being Present through Body Awareness
Lesson 3 Interconnection, Kindness, and Gratitude
Lesson 4 Working with Emotions and Watering Helpful Seeds
Lesson 5 Mindful Speech and Making Healthy Decisions
Lesson 6 Using Technology Mindfully
Lesson 7 Peace
Lesson 8 Final Reflections

LEARNING ACTIVITIES

The unit strives to provide students with an experiential understanding of mindfulness by engaging students in mindfulness practice. Each lesson builds upon the previous one and comes back to the course's essential questions:

What is mindfulness?
How can I be mindful?
Why be mindful?

RESOURCES

Mindful Movements: Ten Exercises for Well-Being by Thich Nhat Hanh
Mindful Teaching and Teaching Mindfulness by Deborah Schoeberlein
Collaborative for Academic, Social and Emotional Learning (http://www.casel.org/)
The Miracle of Mindfulness by Thich Nhat Hanh
Planting Seeds: Practicing Mindfulness with Children by Thich Nhat Hanh and the Plum Village Community

UNIT REFLECTION

Every time I teach this unit, I spend time afterward reflecting on challenges I had to overcome in order to achieve deep understanding. Taking time to reflect and assess is essential to strengthen my ability to make changes so the next time my instruction will be more effective.

CHAPTER FOURTEEN

LESSON ONE: BEING PRESENT THROUGH BREATH AWARENESS

Mindfulness means take a second and just breathe with awareness. Mindfulness to me means something true to my life. It's my true friend. It's the only thing that can make me calm.
—**CHLOE, age 10**

The First Days of School by Harry and Rosemary Wong is a legendary book frequently given to new teachers. I was one of these new teachers and received the following sage guidance from the Wongs twelve years ago: "Your success during the school year will be determined by what you do on the first days of school. . . . Your purpose is to affect lives and effective teachers affect lives."[22] To be effective, you must have strong classroom-management skills. An instructional strategy often cited in promoting social emotional learning is providing students with opportunities to have some say in what happens in the classroom. Developing a shared vision of how the classroom is run increases student buy-in.[23]

As you engage in your first lesson with your students, I cannot stress enough the importance of co-creating a shared set of expectations for your class. Having worked in a progressive school where education is student centered, I've seen the value in developing shared norms and values in the classroom. This process will create a strong foundation for your classroom community to thrive and enable you to more effectively manage your class.

Creating a shared sense of values and norms sets the stage for a restorative, rather than punitive, approach if a discipline issue arises.[24]

For example, when responding to conflict you can employ a restorative approach by asking those involved the following key questions:

1. What happened, and what were you thinking at the time of the incident?
2. What have you thought about since?
3. Who has been affected by what happened, and how?
4. What about this has been the hardest for you?
5. What do you think needs to be done to make things as right as possible?

If you have a shared set of class agreements that all students have bought into, it makes it much easier to engage in the restorative process. Through engaging in these questions you focus on the harm done rather than the rule itself, which helps strengthen and restore relationships. Restorative practices also build capacity around a student's self-management, a critical life skill and one of the Five SEL Core competencies. (See page 90 for a list of the competencies.)

This first lesson sets the tone for the rest of your mindfulness unit and it introduces the foundational practice of mindful breathing. If you are a classroom teacher, even after the unit ends, the hope is that you continuously refer back to the skills taught in your mindfulness unit. For example, you can engage your students in mindful breathing before tests or during transitions to help them refocus. It's important that mindfulness is introduced and framed in an inviting way, and when you first involve your students in creating shared classroom expectations they will have a more vested interest in being a part of classroom activities.

Creating shared classroom expectations requires a bit of "letting go" on the teacher's part. Just as you hold students accountable to the class norms, they hold you accountable. A few years ago, my sixth-grade students were voting for class names and the final choices were crazily inventive: Flying Purple Hippos, Screaming Soup, and the Dark Unicorns of Social Indifference. I was upset that the Dark Unicorns of Social Indifference was in the final three—I couldn't have my "mindful" class be associated with social "indifference." I was sure that my students didn't understand what indifference meant, so during the voting I worked with them to understand the definition. Sure enough, they were mistaken; they thought "indifference" meant people who are "different" were cool and included. I suggested they change the name to Positive Unicorns of Social Justice. After we voted, I was happy to see that Flying Purple Hippos won. But the next day the students came to my teaching partner and me with a petition. A large group of students felt that I lobbied and used my position as the teacher to put down the Dark Unicorns of Social Indifference in my explanation of indifference, and my explanation wasn't aligned with our classroom norms around respectful communication.

We had a class meeting to discuss everyone's concerns. I realized that I could have handled the voting in a much more skillful and honest way, apologized to my students for lobbying, and thoughtfully explained why I felt uncomfortable with the word indifference. As a class we decided to have a revote but remove "indifference" as an option once everyone understood what it meant, and in the end, we were called the Screaming Soup. I share this story because initially, letting go of some control to create a sense of shared involvement with young people can be scary. However, I'm a firm believer that it's the only way to create authentic relationships; mindfulness is not about controlling yourself and others, it's about bringing more authenticity into our lives, but doing so in a skillful way.

Stage One—Desired Results

SUMMARY

The purpose of this lesson is to introduce students to mindfulness practice through breath awareness.

ENDURING UNDERSTANDINGS

Students will understand: Being mindful can help me manage my life more effectively.

ESSENTIAL QUESTIONS

Why be mindful?
What is mindfulness?
How can I be mindful?

KNOWLEDGE CONTENT

Students know:

- Whenever your mind becomes scattered, you can use your breath to come back to yourself.
- You can use mindfulness to calm yourself, reduce stress, work skillfully with strong emotions, and maintain focus.
- Mindfulness enables us to consciously repattern our brain towards an improved mental, emotional, and physical state.

SKILLS

Students will be able to:

- Recognize when they are not present.
- Keep the mind focused by using the breath as an anchor.
- Use their breath to connect their body and mind.

Stage Two — Assessment Evidence

In each class students are asked to reflect on the mindfulness practices they are learning by answering orally or in written form the three essential questions: Why be mindful? What is mindfulness? How can I be mindful?

Class discussion about the importance of paying attention and developing concentration relates to students understanding the importance of assuming responsibility for personal health behaviors. Their participation in mindfulness practices demonstrates healthy behaviors.

In this lesson, students are asked to focus on a still object for thirty seconds and note when their mind slips to the past or future. They do this before learning how breath awareness can anchor them in the present moment and build concentration. For homework they have to breathe mindfully for one minute and try the exercise again to see if their concentration improves. Through the lesson they are assessing their ability to concentrate for thirty seconds, learning a new strategy and then seeing if it improves concentration.

Stage Three — Learning Plan

Before Class Begins: *Teacher Meditation*

As course instructor, you meditate during the five to ten minutes before class begins because the most important thing in being with and teaching children is one's state of mind. Your presence is the greatest gift you can offer your students. When you are solid, happy, and full of love and compassion, you will naturally know how to create a happy classroom environment and how to water the positive qualities in your students. If you are not at peace, you cannot impart that energy to your class. Each lesson is preceded by a teacher meditation accompanied by a gatha poem. Read each line to yourself as you breathe in and out.

Exercise one from *The Blooming of a Lotus* by Thich Nhat Hanh[25]

Joy of Meditation as Nourishment
Breathing-in, I calm my body.
Calm
Breathing-out, I smile.
Smile
Breathing-in, I dwell in Present moment
the present moment
Breathing-out, I know it is Wonderful moment
a wonderful moment.

1. Classroom setup

Seating is organized in a circle with desks on the outside.

2. Greet students at the door with your attendance sheet—mindfully take attendance

Make eye contact with each student, smile, ask them their name, welcome them to class, mark attendance, and hand them a course description as they enter. Direct students to take a seat.

3. Once the school bell rings, close your eyes, breathe deeply and invite the mindfulness bell

See what the reactions of students are. Explain to students that the focus of this class is helping us understand and train our minds and the mindfulness bell is a tool we use to do that. Tell them we will return to the bell later on in class.

4. Discussion time

Ask students what "harmony" means. Guide students toward a shared understanding of this word and then ask: Why is it important to have harmony in the classroom?

Repeat and rephrase student responses.

5. Shared norms

Tell students that before we can really learn together we have to spend some time creating shared guidelines for our class. Everyone will have a chance to offer one guideline to help our class be in harmony. Offer the first guideline as the golden rule ("Treat others as you would like to be treated"), what you feel is the guiding principle for our classroom with respect to how we treat each other. Be firm but friendly about not tolerating any disrespect.

Have each student share one guideline each and write them down on poster paper. When you are finished, have each student sign the poster paper. Keep this poster paper up during all of your classes; you can refer back to it if a class member isn't following the shared expectations.

6. Discuss: "The present is a gift"[26]

If you have access to the film *Kung Fu Panda*, there is a great clip/quote to open your teaching of mindfulness. If you don't have access to the film, you can still share the quote below and reference the film:

> There is a saying: "Yesterday is history, tomorrow is a mystery, but today is a gift. That is why it is called the 'present.'"

Ask them what the clip means and guide them to answer the question: Why is it important to be in the present? Relate this question to paying attention and why it might be important for school and life.

7. Share that mindfulness is a skill that can help us be in the present

Ask students: What is a skill? Can you improve a skill? How?

Share with students that during the next seven classes they are going to learn more about a potentially very important life skill—mindfulness.

8. Benefits of practicing mindfulness

Share that Phil Jackson, former LA Lakers coach, uses mindfulness to assist his players in paying exact attention to what is happening on the court moment by moment. He teaches players mindfulness so they can relax more fully. Mindfulness allows his players to make the correct decisions during extremely tense and chaotic times on the basketball court. If you have time, share Phil Jackson's thoughts on mindfulness with your students:

> Like life, basketball is messy and unpredictable. It has its way with you, no matter how hard you try to control it. The trick is to experience each moment with a clear mind and open heart. When you do that, the game—and life—will take care of itself.[27]

List the skills you will learn: maintain/focus attention; work skillfully with our emotions; manage stress; develop a sense of inner peace; promote compassion and kindness toward oneself and others; be resilient; recognize interdependence/interconnection; foster understanding; communicate effectively; make healthy decisions. Share with students how research and your own experiences have helped you in the above ways and, because you believe in sharing what has improved your life, you want to share mindfulness with them. If you have a short but compelling story about how mindfulness has helped you, now would be a great time to share it.

9. Mindfulness and the brain

Hebb's Rule: "Neurons that fire together, wire together." Share how in our brains, connections among the neurons are "plastic" and can change throughout our lives. The more we practice mindfulness just as with any other skill we can improve our ability to stay focused, remain calm in challenging situations, and increase understanding of ourselves and others. (For more background on mindfulness and the brain I suggest reading some of Rick Hanson's work, detailed in the Recommended Resources section of the book.)

Introduce students to two important parts of their brain, the amygdala and the prefrontal cortex. Self-management is reinforced as students learn that when their amygdala is fired up, they can't access their prefrontal cortex to make a thoughtful decision. You can fill a clear plastic bottle with water and glitter and shake it to represent an experience of a strong emotion or high stress when our amygdala is reacting. Once the shaking stops, have students breathe mindfully as the glitter settles down to the bottom. This represents that as we settle down we are able to make better decisions.

10. Attitude is everything

The next seven classes are about you (the students) trying to give yourselves the gift of being more relaxed as a way of being kind to your own mind, of finding how you can look after and train your mind in ways that are incredibly helpful to you and that can bring you a lot of happiness. Frame this unit as an invitation, but stress that the attitude they bring to class every day can really impact what they get out of the unit.

11. Balance task

Ask for two students to balance one book each on their heads while standing on one foot. When they finish ask them to share with the class what was happening as they tried to balance the book—guide them to share, for example, they had to focus, pay attention, etc.

12. Paying attention

Have students focus on a still object for 30 seconds and have them note when their mind slips to the past or future. At this point, hand them their mindfulness journal, which recaps the lesson and has their homework. Students note in their journal how often they are not fully present during the thirty seconds. Debrief the exercise and discuss how our minds tend to wander and that our attention doesn't stay put even if we want it to.

13. The breath is your best friend

Share with students that the most effective way we can bring our mind back to the present moment is by paying attention to our breath. We can't breathe in the future or the past, only in the present.

14. Belly breathing

Check to make sure all of the students are comfortable. Then share that you are going to invite a bell of mindfulness. If students feel safe, they can close their eyes. *Think of the sound of the bell as the voice of a loved one that only wants you to be happy and peaceful. When we hear the bell we stop what we are doing and take time to breathe and enjoy ourselves.* Before inviting the bell you may want students to identify their breathing by asking them to put their finger horizontally under their nose. What does their breath feel like?

Stress that while we breathe all the time we are usually not aware of it. What would happen to us if we couldn't breathe?

Ask the students: "Put your hand on your belly and notice what happens when you breathe." Have them follow their breathing for a few moments in silence.

Now ask them how they feel when they just pay attention to their breathing. It may be beneficial to now share how mindful breathing has helped you.

Now have students notice how long their in-breath lasts and how many seconds their out-breath lasts. Now count how many breaths you take during one interval between bell soundings. Introduce them to the Plum Village mindfulness bell gatha: When we breathe in, we say, "*Listen, listen,*" and when we breathe out, "*This wonderful sound brings me back to my true home.*" We all have a peaceful space inside of us that we can always go back to—it's always there. Slowly guide students out of the exercise.

15. You should know how to breathe, in order to maintain mindfulness

Whenever you find that your mind has wandered, you can use your breath to take hold of your mind again. We can use our breath as a tool to build up the power of concentration, which comes from practicing mindfulness.

16. Ask students: How can you use your breathing to practice mindfulness?

17. When training your mind, be gentle. It's all about learning a new skill

Stress the importance of kindness toward oneself. Approach this unit as an opportunity to discover and understand your mind and know yourself better.

For homework assignments and handout materials related to lesson one, see the appendix , page 184.

CHAPTER FIFTEEN

LESSON TWO: BEING PRESENT THROUGH BODY AWARENESS

A FEW YEARS AGO I had the chance to hear Mihaly Csikszentmihalyi, author of *Flow: The Psychology of Optimal Experience*, speak at the Brain Development and Learning Conference in Vancouver. I had heard of the term "flow," an experience in which you are completely absorbed in the activity at hand, well before I heard of mindfulness. Prior to learning about mindfulness, my most tangible experiences of complete presence involved sports because I was fully present in my body.

This lesson helps your students to access the present moment through body awareness and introduces them to the key mindfulness practices of mindful walking, mindful movements, and deep relaxation. Once your students are familiar with bringing awareness to their bodies, you can invite them to bring their attention to their physical sensations throughout the day. For example, the next time they pick up a pencil, invite them to do it with awareness. What do they feel in their arms, their hands, or their fingers when they pick up the pencil? What do they feel in their bodies when they write? Try to find moments throughout the day to invite your students back into their bodies.

Students are also taught how to use a "talking piece" as used in restorative justice circles and listen actively to each other in a circle. The circle process is a great structure for class meetings, restorative practice, and building community. Even when you are not formally teaching mindfulness, a circle (be sure students rotate spots) is an extremely powerful, inclusive way to physically structure your classroom set up.

Stage One—Desired Results

SUMMARY

The purpose of this lesson is to teach students how to be present through body awareness.

ENDURING UNDERSTANDINGS

Students will understand: Being mindful can help me manage my life more effectively.

ESSENTIAL QUESTIONS

Why be mindful?
What is mindfulness?
How can I be mindful?

KNOWLEDGE CONTENT

Students know:

- Whenever your mind becomes scattered, you can use your breath and your steps to come back to yourself.
- You can use mindfulness to calm yourself, reduce stress, work skillfully with strong emotions, and maintain focus.

- Mindfulness enables us to consciously repattern our brain toward an improved mental, emotional, and physical state.

SKILLS

Students will be able to:

- Recognize when they are not present.
- Keep the mind focused by using the breath and steps as an anchor.
- Utilize various practices to balance the mind such as moving the attention from one body part to another (mindful movements, simple stretches, deep relaxation).

Stage Two — Assessment Evidence

In each class, students are asked to reflect on the mindfulness practices they are learning by answering orally or in written form the three essential questions: Why be mindful? What is mindfulness? How can I be mindful?

In this lesson, students are asked to walk mindfully in order to help cultivate greater attention, focus, and awareness. For homework they have to practice walking mindfully. Through the lesson they are learning another strategy to promote awareness, focus, and concentration. Students are also guided through a deep relaxation exercise and reflect on how this practice makes them feel. In the next class, they will discuss which practices, if any, they find useful and try to incorporate them.

Stage Three — Learning Plan

LEARNING ACTIVITIES

Before Class Begins: *Teacher Meditation*

Exercise two from *The Blooming of a Lotus* by Thich Nhat Hanh[28]

Joy of Meditation as Nourishment

1. *Breathing in, I know I am breathing in.*
   In
   Breathing out, I know I am breathing out.
   Out
2. *Breathing in, my breath grows deep.*
   Deep
   Breathing out, my breath goes slowly.
   Slow
3. *Aware of my body, I breathe in. Aware of body*
   Relaxing my body, I breathe out. Relaxing body
4. *Calming my body, I breathe in. Calming my body*
   Caring for my body, I breathe out. Caring for body
5. *Smiling to my body, I breathe in. Smiling to body*
   Easing my body, I breathe-out. Easing body
6. *Smiling to my body, I breathe in. Smiling to body*
   Releasing the tensions in my body, I
   breathe out. Releasing tensions
7. *Feeling joy (to be alive), I breathe in. Feeling joy*
   Feeling happy, I breathe-out. Feeling happy
8. *Dwelling in the present moment, I*
   breathe in. Being present
   Enjoying the present moment, I breathe out. Enjoying
9. *Aware of my stable posture, I breathe in. Stable posture*
   Enjoying the stability, I breathe out. Enjoying

1. Classroom setup/set up mindful walking outside
Seating is organized in a circle with desks on the outside.

2. Greet students at the door with your attendance sheet—mindfully take attendance
Make eye contact with each student, smile, welcome them to class, give them any handouts for that day, mark attendance, and tell them to stand in the circle.

3. Being present through body awareness
Share that today's class will focus on being present through building awareness of our bodies.

4. Invite the bell and do mindful movements
Share your ten favorite stretches with your students. Before they begin stretching make sure they create an invisible circle around themselves that designates their own individual practice space. When engaging in mindfulness activities it will be important to remind them of their invisible circle to create a safe space for practices.

Have them coordinate their breathing with each movement. An inhale usually coordinates when the movement leads to your body getting larger and an exhale when it gets smaller. For example, inhale as your raise your arms up and exhale as you lower them down. I usually draw on Thich Nhat Hanh's *Mindful Movements: Ten Exercises for Well-Being.*[29]

5. Talking Circle practice
You will now introduce students to a Talking Circle and tell them that from now on in every class we will come together as a community to share our reflections on what we are learning and discovering. When we come together like this it's called Talking Circle.

You can also guide your students to come up with another name for the Talking Circle. One year my students called it, "Circle of Love, Peace, and Power." During our Talking Circle we all practice mindful listening and show mutual respect by using a talking piece so that only one person speaks at a time. When that person holds the talking piece, the rest of the circle listens actively. You can use any item for a talking piece from a rock to a feather. Just make sure the talking piece isn't something that could draw attention away from your students. In years past, I've used the inviter for inviting the mindfulness bell as the talking piece. When introducing the talking piece, it is helpful to give them the history of the talking stick and the use of circles in human societies and to explain that such circles have been used for centuries by many indigenous cultures to discuss important matters, resolve conflicts, and promote peace.

This would be a good time to talk about what it means to be respectful and to listen actively.

6. Ask students to share a reflection from one of their homework assignments, and each student holds the talking piece as they share

For all future mindfulness-focused classes students will be given an opportunity to share and reflect from their homework assignments in the Talking Circle.

7. Introducing mindful walking

Share with students that today we are going to experience being present through body awareness. If possible take them outside, especially if your classroom space is small.

Remind students of their invisible circle practice space and how it goes with them wherever they go, protecting them and keeping them safe while they practice.

First have students walk normally for thirty seconds. Then have them walk as if they were upset for thirty seconds, excited for thirty seconds, and continue on for at least two minutes and up to three minutes having students represent various states as they walk. Finally, have them walk while maintaining focus. Then ask them why they think you offered this activity. Guide students toward sharing how our feelings and body are connected and how we show our emotions in our posture and way of walking. You can ask them how they think their body, feelings, and emotions are connected.

8. Walking with their own gatha

Now, introduce the concept of mindful walking. Speak from your own experience about what mindful walking means to you and model how you practice it. Usually I share my story from Mount Kailash detailed earlier in this book.

First have each student choose one positive word like "happy," "joyful," "or peaceful."

Model coordinating each in-breath with your step and the word, and do the same with your out-breath. Take eight steps. Then have the students do it for sixteen steps. Make sure they have space to walk freely and remind them to coordinate their breath and word with each step.

If possible, you can also teach them how to bring awareness to the sensations of each part of their feet from their toes to their heels as they place their feet on the ground.

9. Deep relaxation

When you return to the classroom, have students lie down on their backs and guide them through a deep relaxation. Note that it is very important that you work with the school counselor when sharing this practice with students who have experienced trauma. A great resource for working with students who have experienced trauma is Trauma Sensitive Schools (www.traumasensitiveschools.org).

Read the following script slowly and take a few breaths after each sentence so you can create a comfortable pace for the deep relaxation. You can invite a bell at the beginning and end of the deep relaxation to help students maintain a more relaxed state. You will find a version of this script in the appendix that you can copy and share with your students.

Take some time now to get very comfortable on your back. Congratulate yourself because you are now taking some very important time just for you to relax. This is time we rarely spend in our busy lives. Once you are in a comfortable position, gently close your eyes and, if you can, bring a half smile to your face. Now bring awareness to your breathing. If it is helpful you can place one hand on your chest and one on your belly, and you can feel your belly and chest rise and fall as you breathe. With each breath in and out, silently count to yourself, *One, two, three . . .*

As you breathe, feel your body on the floor and sink deep into the ground; you are safe; you are protected. Inhaling and exhaling, inhaling and exhaling, you relax your whole body, relax your whole body. Breathing in and breathing out, your whole body feels weightless, as if you are floating on the water or a fluffy cloud.

You have nowhere to be but right here, relaxing with your breath, no worries, no tension, just breathing in and breathing out.

Breathing in, bring awareness to your arms. Breathing out, release any tension you may have in your arms all the way down to your hands. Breathing in, bring awareness to your hands; breathing out, focus on your right hand. As you breathe, bring your awareness to each finger—thumb, index finger, middle finger, ring finger, pinky. Breathing in, focus on the palm of your right hand; breathing out, relax your entire hand. Now bring awareness to your left hand. Breathing in, focus on each finger—thumb, index finger, middle finger, ring finger, pinky. Breathing in, focus on the palm of your left hand, breathing out relax your entire hand. Now breathe deeply and send love and gratitude to both of your hands. Our hands make it possible for us to draw, play sports, cook, and so much more. Our hands are very precious.

Breathing in, bring your awareness to your legs. Breathing out, relax your legs completely. As you move your awareness down your right leg, release any tension you may feel from your thighs to your knees to your calves, down to your ankles and finally to your right foot. Breathing in and out, big toe, second toe, middle toe, fourth toe, pinky toe. Breathing in, bring awareness to your left leg. Breathing out, as you move your awareness down your left leg, release any tension you may feel from your thighs to your knees to your calves, down to your ankles and finally to your left foot. Now bring awareness to each toe on your left foot. Breathing in and out, big toe, second toe, middle toe, fourth toe, pinky toe. Wiggle your toes as you release and relax your feet. Our feet bring us so much joy; they make it possible to skip, play soccer, and dance. Send love and gratitude to your feet.

Now move up your body to the top of your head. Breathing in and out, release any tension you may have in your forehead. Take a few breaths as you relax the muscles around your head and feel the weight of your head on the ground. Now, breathing in, bring awareness to your eyes, allow your eyes to completely relax, and, breathing out, release any tension you may have around your eyes. Our eyes bring so much beauty to sight; we are so grateful for our eyes. Now send love to your eyes and let them rest.

Breathing in, bring your awareness to your mouth. Breathing out, allow your mouth to relax. Release any tension you have around your mouth. Perhaps you still have that gentle half smile on your face—did you know that smiling releases the tension in the hundreds of muscles in your face? Feel the tension release as you smile. Our mouths enable us to eat, sing, and take in fresh air. Send love and thanks to your mouth.

Now breathing in, bring your awareness to your shoulders. Breathing out, allow your shoulders to completely release and relax. Let all the tension in your shoulders release into the floor and exit your body. Breathing in, send care to your shoulders; breathing out, send your shoulders love.

Breathing in, bring your awareness to your heart. Breathing out, allow your heart to relax. Our hearts work so hard 24/7, but we forget to recognize our hearts and send them love. With each breath, embrace your heart with kindness, gratitude, and love. Silently thank your heart for all it does to keep you alive.

[Play relaxing music for some minutes.]

Bring your awareness back to your breathing . . . to your belly rising and falling. Following your breathing, become aware of your arms and legs. You can now stretch if you'd like, and when you feel ready, slowly sit up. You can stretch more and, when you feel ready, slowly and mindfully stand up.

In this exercise you can use any part of the body: the hair, the ears, the nose, lungs, internal organs, the digestive system, or any part of the body that needs healing and care. Just embrace each part with mindfulness and gratitude as you hold it in your awareness and breathe in and out.

10. Unit essential questions

End class by returning to the unit essential questions: Why be mindful? What is mindfulness? How can I be mindful? Have students reflect on what they learned in this class and connect it to unit essential questions.

11. Homework

- Practice gatha walking for at least thirty steps and write about it in your journal.
- Do deep relaxation at least once between now and our next class and write about it in your journal. A good time to do deep relaxation is before bed or whenever you are feeling tired. You can have a parent read the script in your homework for you, or you can try doing it yourself by first bringing awareness to belly breathing and consciously breathing as you relax parts of your body.

For more homework, handout materials, and a script you can use to teach deep relaxation, see pages 188 to 192 in the appendix.

CHAPTER SIXTEEN

LESSON THREE: INTERCONNECTION, KINDNESS, AND GRATITUDE

ONE OF THE MOST powerful teachings I came across during my five years living in India was that of Indra's Net. A metaphor for the universe, Indra's Net is depicted as a net of fathomless proportions and at each point of intersection a jewel that represents an individual life form reflects all of the other countless jewels in the net. Each jewel reflects the infinity of jewels. In one jewel, you see all jewels and everything comes out of this web of life. Nothing stands alone; we all live in each other.

The purpose of this lesson is to help students begin to experience the sense of interconnectedness described in Indra's Net. Through practicing mindful eating, they reflect on the infinite causes and conditions that bring their food to their mouths. Students also think deeply about interconnection and the beneficial role kindness and gratitude can play in their lives.

Looking deeply into interconnection, kindness, and gratitude with young people can be a heartening experience. In 2010 when I engaged in teacher research through following a group of students in my class as they learned mindfulness, I was deeply moved by their response to the mindfulness lessons I taught them. Teacher research is an academic reflective practice that really looks at "the teacher" as the central figure of change or transformation, and through this process these children in the study became my mindfulness teachers. To this day, their candid remarks on kindness, gratitude, and interconnection warm my heart. While reciprocity did appear as a theme in their interviews, the subjects also expressed a deepening understanding. One student said, "When I do something kind it feels like glitter is touching my heart." Being kind is a win-win for everyone and it makes everyone feel good!

Stage One — Desired Results

SUMMARY

The purpose of this lesson is to develop experiential understanding of interconnection and interdependence and have students reflect on kindness and gratitude.

ENDURING UNDERSTANDINGS

Students will understand: Being mindful can help me manage my life more effectively.

ESSENTIAL QUESTIONS:

Why be mindful?
What is mindfulness?
How can I be mindful?

KNOWLEDGE CONTENT

Students know:

- The concept of Interbeing
- Definitions of kindness and gratitude

SKILLS

Students will be able to:

- Eat with awareness.
- Reflect on the factors that contribute to their food's existence.

Stage Two — Assessment Evidence

In each class, students are asked to reflect on the mindfulness practices they are learning by answering orally or in written form the three essential questions: Why be mindful? What is mindfulness? How can I be mindful? In this lesson, students are asked to eat mindfully in order to help cultivate greater awareness of what they put in their bodies. For homework they have to practice mindfully eating one meal and reflect on the experience. Through the lesson, they are learning another strategy to promote awareness of food intake. Students also learn the "smiling strategy" and are asked to try it out and see how it works for them.

Stage Three — Learning Plan

LEARNING ACTIVITIES

Before Class Begins: *Teacher Meditation*

From the first part of Exercise eleven in *The Blooming of a Lotus* by Thich Nhat Hanh:[30]

> **Being in Touch Looking Deeply**
>
> *In touch with the flower, I breathe in.*
>
> *Flower*
>
> *In touch with the scent and beauty*

of the flower, I breathe out.
beauty and scent
In touch with the sun in the flower, I breathe in.
Sun in the flower
Knowing without the sun there would
be no flower, I breathe out.
without sun, no flower

In touch with the cloud in the flower, I breathe in.
cloud in the flower
Knowing without the cloud there would
be no flower, I breathe out.
without cloud, no flower

If possible, try to eat or drink mindfully before class.

1. Classroom setup

Seating is organized in a circle with desks on the outside.

2. Greet students at the door with your attendance sheet—mindfully take attendance

Make eye contact with each student, smile, welcome them to class, give them their handouts for that day, mark attendance, and tell them to go to their seats.

3. Smiling strategy

Begin class with inviting the bell and introduce them to the smiling strategy. Have students close their eyes, follow the sound of the bell, and bring a smile to their face. Inhale and exhale three breaths gently while maintaining the smile. Follow the breath. Play Pachelbel's *Canon* or any other soothing classical music of your choice and have them smile while listening to music. Smile while watching your breathing in and breathing out. Slowly guide them out of the practice. If you find that students have difficulty concentrating while they are engaging in mindful breathing, have them create a circle where they face outward instead of inward, so that they aren't distracted easily by their classmates.

Tell them that their homework will be to smile during their free moments. Anywhere they find themselves sitting or standing, smile. Inhale and exhale quietly three times. They should also smile when irritated. *When you realize you are irritated, smile at once. Breathe in and out quietly while keeping the smile for three breaths.*

4. Talking Circle—everyone share one homework response, use talking piece

5. As a class, read Thich Nhat Hanh's explanation of Interbeing below—use excerpts accordingly depending on the age group you are working with.

> If you are a poet, you will see clearly that there is a cloud floating in this sheet of paper. Without a cloud, there will be no rain; without rain, the trees cannot grow; and without trees, we cannot make paper. The cloud is essential for the paper to exist. If the cloud is not here, the sheet of paper cannot be here either. So we can say that the cloud and the paper inter-are. "Interbeing" is a word that is not in the dictionary yet, but if we combine the prefix "inter-" with the verb "to be," we have a new verb, inter-be. If we look into this sheet of paper even more deeply, we can see the sunshine in it. If the sunshine is not there, the forest cannot grow. In fact, nothing can grow. Even we cannot grow without sunshine. And so, we know that the sunshine is also in this sheet of paper. The paper and the sunshine inter-are. And if we

continue to look, we can see the logger who cut the tree and brought it to the mill to be transformed into paper. And we see the wheat. We know the logger cannot exist without his daily bread, and therefore the wheat that became his bread is also in this sheet of paper. And the logger's father and mother are in it too.

When we look in this way, we see that without all of these things, this sheet of paper cannot exist. Looking even more deeply, we can see we are in it too. This is not difficult to see, because when we look at a sheet of paper, the sheet of paper is part of our perception. Your mind is in here and mine is also. So we can say that everything is in here with this sheet of paper. You cannot point out one thing that is not here—time, space, the earth, the rain, the minerals in the soil, the sunshine, the cloud, the river, the heat.

Everything coexists with this sheet of paper. That is why I think the word inter-be should be in the dictionary. "To be" is to inter-be. You cannot just be by yourself alone. You have to inter-be with every other thing. This sheet of paper is, because everything else is. Suppose we try to return one of the elements to its source. Suppose we return the sunshine to the sun. Do you think that this sheet of paper will be possible? No, without sunshine nothing can be. And if we return the logger to his mother, then we have no sheet of paper either. The fact is that this sheet of paper is made up only of "non-paper elements." And if we return these non-paper elements to their sources, then there can be no paper at all. Without "non-paper elements," like mind, logger, sunshine and so on, there will be no paper. As thin as this sheet of paper is, it contains everything in the universe in it.[31]

6. Facilitate a class discussion about Interbeing

Ask students to describe what they think Interbeing means. Push them to explain their thinking and provide examples to foster a rich discussion.

7. Mindful eating

Hand each student a small item of food (e.g., an almond or a raisin) and have them eat it normally. Then hand them a second small item of food and guide them through mindful eating. They first observe the food and slowly savor it, paying attention to the taste and the sensation of eating. As you do this, ask questions about the origin of the food and make connections to Interbeing.

Have them write in their journals about the difference between eating the food normally vs. mindfully. Introduce them to the adaptation below of the Plum Village food contemplations and have them comment on the contemplations as they are read.

> *This food is the gift of the whole universe: the*
> *earth, the sky, the rain, and the sun.*
>
> *We thank the people who have made this food, especially*
> *the farmers, the people at the market and the cooks.*
>
> *We only put on our plate as much food as we can eat.*
>
> *We want to chew the food slowly so that we*
> *can enjoy it more and digest it better.*
>
> *This food gives us energy to practice being*
> *more loving and understanding.*
>
> *We eat this food in order to be healthy and*
> *happy, and to love each other as a family.*

8. Kindness

Ask students to define kindness. Write up the definitions they offer and try to come up with a shared classroom understanding of what kindness is. You may want to share what kindness means to you and be sure to speak to how we can be kind to others and not just ourselves.

9. Metta

Now you can introduce them to the Pali word *metta*. "Metta" is a Pali word that means loving kindness and friendliness toward oneself and others. Even though this is a word traditionally used in Buddhist settings, I introduce it to students by talking about why the NBA player Metta World Peace, formerly known as Ronald William Artest, Jr., changed his name to Metta. Back when he was Ron Artest, he was part of an infamous brawl when he went into the stands and punched a fan—his name change signaled a new path of peace. Metta's publicist said he had been thinking about the switch for years. "It took many years of research and soul-searching to find a first name that was both personally meaningful and inspirational. Changing my name was meant to inspire and bring youth together all around the world," World Peace said in a statement released after his name change hearing.[32]

Invite the bell and lead students through a kindness reflection or more traditional metta practice.

- May I touch happiness
- May I live in peace
- May I always feel embraced by love

Now ask them to choose one person to send kindness from their heart to

- May my loved ones touch happiness and feel joy
- May my loved ones live in peace
- May my loved ones always feel embraced by love

You can have them send love to those suffering as well.

If you think it's appropriate and you have time, you can engage them in a discussion of whether it is possible to love someone but not their actions. Talk about how everyone just wants to be happy and how this desire connects us. You can also encourage them to partake in stealth kindness, where you send kindness to individuals you may not know personally, to the passengers in the car next to you while driving, in line at the grocery store, and so on.

10. Gratitude

Now invite your students to define gratitude. Share with them that a strategy for feeling happy is to reflect on all of the things they are grateful for. Encourage students to reflect on what they are grateful for before they go to bed and when they wake up in the morning. If time permits, lead them through a gratitude meditation in which they *feel* what they are grateful for. Have each student make a gratitude card listing what they are grateful for and encourage them to really connect with the feelings they have when writing down each item they are grateful for and savoring those feelings. You can even have them first start listing nouns they are grateful for followed by verbs and finally items they are grateful for connected to the web of life detailed in chapter eleven.

11. Unit essential questions

End class by returning to the unit essential questions: Why be mindful? What is mindfulness? How can I be mindful? Have students reflect on what they learned in this class and connect it to unit essential questions.

12. Interbeing artistic responses

Have students spend the rest of the period creating artistic responses to the Thich Nhat Hanh reading.

13. **Go over homework**
    - Smile during your free moments. Anywhere you find yourself sitting or standing, smile. When you realize you are annoyed or upset, smile and see what happens. Write about the smiling strategy in your journals.
    - Eat one food item mindfully before our next class and write about it in your journal.
    - Complete your Interbeing artistic response if you didn't finish it in class.
    - Reflect on what you are grateful for each night before you go to bed.

For a handout and homework assignments related to lesson three, see pages 193 to 195 in the appendix.

CHAPTER SEVENTEEN

LESSON FOUR: WORKING WITH EMOTIONS AND WATERING HELPFUL SEEDS

Every day I water a helpful seed in my mom when I tell her I love her and then a helpful seed goes in her and in me.
—CARINA

A Cherokee elder told his grandson that there is a battle between two wolves inside us all. One wolf is hatred, greed, anger, and jealousy, and the other wolf is kindness, peace, love, and generosity. When the elder's grandson asked, "Who wins?" his grandfather replied, "Whichever one you feed."

"Two Wolves" is a popular Native American legend that was first introduced to me by an exceptional elementary school teacher named Jann Fling. When one of my mindfulness classes got to the lesson of working with emotions and watering helpful seeds, the students who had been in Jann's class in fifth grade would say, "Wow, Ms. Srinivasan, this is just like the 'two wolves' Ms. Fling told us about!"

This lesson helps students see that inside of us we have both helpful and unhelpful seeds of emotion like the two wolves, and whatever seeds we choose to water, those are the seeds that will grow. Mindfulness helps us develop awareness of the seeds we are watering so we can grow more helpful seeds. This lesson also introduces a helpful strategy created by Sister Chau Nghiem (Jewel) of the Plum Village monastic community for working with strong emotions called BCOOL, which was introduced in chapter seven.

BCOOL stands for **B**reathe,
Calm yourself down,
know that the situation is **O**kay,
Observe what's happening inside,
and hold it with **L**ove.

Stage One — Desired Results

SUMMARY

The purpose of this lesson is to teach students how to take care of strong emotions when they arise.

ENDURING UNDERSTANDINGS

Students will understand: Being mindful can help me manage my life more effectively.

ESSENTIAL QUESTIONS

Why be mindful?
What is mindfulness?
How can I be mindful?

KNOWLEDGE CONTENT

Students know:

- The concept of "watering seeds."

SKILLS

Students will be able to:

- Identify and label emotions and feelings.
- Use "watering seeds" to practice self-management.
- Use the BCOOL strategy to work with challenging emotions.

Stage Two — Assessment Evidence

In each class, students are asked to reflect on the mindfulness practices they are learning by answering orally or in written form the three essential questions: Why be mindful? What is mindfulness? How can I be mindful?

Class discussion about the importance of cultivating awareness and managing their emotions relates to students understanding the importance of assuming responsibility for personal health behaviors. Their participation in mindfulness practices demonstrates healthy behaviors.

In this lesson, students examine how they manage and work with their emotions. They are given the strategy of watering helpful seeds in themselves and others and are asked to apply this strategy to situations.

Stage Three — Learning Plan

LEARNING ACTIVITIES

Before Class Begins: *Teacher Meditation*

Adapted from Exercise Four in *The Blooming of a Lotus* by Thich Nhat Hanh:[33]

Looking Deeply

Aware of my mental health, I breathe in,
Aware of Mental Health
Smiling to the state of my mental health, I breathe out,
Smiling
Seeing unwholesome seeds in me, I breathe in,
Unwholesome Seeds
Determined not to water these seeds anymore

and transform them, I breathe out.
Transform

(Feel free to substitute unhelpful for unwholesome in the meditation.)

1. Classroom setup

Seating is organized in a circle with desks on the outside.

2. Greet students at the door with your attendance sheet—mindfully take attendance

Make eye contact with each student, smile, welcome them to class, give them any handouts for that day, mark attendance, and tell them to lie down somewhere in the room.

3. Belly breathing lying down

Have students lie down flat on their backs (remind them of their invisible circles) and invite the bell. Instruct them to keep their arms loose by their sides and their legs slightly apart.

> Gently close your eyes and bring a smile to your face. Breathe in and out gently, holding your attention on your full inhale and full exhale. Sink each part of your body down into the floor and let go entirely. Place one hand on your belly and bring awareness to the rising and falling of your abdomen with each breath. Continue for ten breaths.

Slowly guide students out of belly breathing and have them gather in a circle.

4. Talking Circle—everyone shares one reflection from their homework using the talking piece

As students share you can invite them to also check in with the group around how they are feeling emotionally. I usually ask students to hold up a number of fingers depending on how they feel: one finger for really bad and five fingers for great. This way I know who to check in with one-on-one. This can also be a great segue to the class topic for today.

5. Working with emotions

After students share their reflections from homework, tell them that today we are going to focus on working skillfully with strong emotions. Ask students, "What are emotions?" Guide them toward a shared understanding of emotions. Make sure the definition includes that they are feelings that can be felt in our mind and body and their intensity and length vary. An emotion itself can feel painful, but the way in which we relate to the emotion results in the extent to which it causes suffering. Ask students how they relate to emotions like sadness or anger. Stress that no emotion is bad, but if we don't learn to take care of strong emotions, it could result in a harmful consequence. If you have an example from your life on how you dealt unskillfully with a strong emotion, you can share this experience.

Share that through understanding our emotions we can respond intelligently when they arise. We can't avoid having painful emotions but we can learn how to deal with them.

6. Strategy for Working With Emotions: BCOOL (from Sister Chau Nghiem)

BREATHE: Take three deep breaths. Your breath helps you create awareness of what is happening in the here and now.

CALM: Your breath can also help you calm yourself.

OKAY: Once you calm yourself down you'll know that you are ultimately okay and that whatever you are facing is workable. We need to be able to accept whatever we are experiencing.

OBSERVE: Once you feel better you can observe the emotion while it is happening. Naming the emotion can help it feel less overwhelming. "I'm feeling anger right now." Whatever the emotion is, try to experience it fully. Don't judge it; there's nothing wrong with it. Once you have labeled and accepted the emotion as it is, ask yourself, "What do I feel in my body?" "Why is this emotion there?"

LOVE: Using your breath, hold yourself with love. Be kind to yourself when you experience a challenging emotion. If it is still too overwhelming, try to turn your attention to your breath. You are not trying to ignore your emotion; you are trying to see it clearly. Through clearly seeing your emotion you will take it less personally.

7. Acceptance

Acceptance is the foundation of mindfulness practice. In order to be mindful of anything one needs to accept what's happening and not push it away, even if it is unpleasant. We practice mindfulness to understand why we feel the way we do and learn how we can work with that feeling to ease our own pain and suffering.

8. Watering Seeds

Explain that inside we have all kinds of seeds, but we can build mindfulness and try to water the helpful seeds in ourselves and others more than the unhelpful seeds. In order to do this, we first must have awareness of which seeds are coming up, which ones we are watering, and only then can we act in a more skillful way. Give examples from your own life on how this strategy works. Ask for student examples of watering good seeds in themselves and others and give an example from your own life!

9. Mindfulness helps us become aware of what seeds we are watering!

Using an example from your own life, talk about how mindfulness can help us become aware of what seeds we are watering.

10. Essential Questions

End class by returning to the unit's essential questions: Why be mindful? What is mindfulness? How can I be mindful? Have students reflect on what they learned in this class and connect it to the essential questions.

11. Homework

- Observe yourself closely before our next class and reflect on the ways in which you work with strong emotions. Do you react to them? Suppress them?
- Next time a strong emotion comes up, practice BCOOL. What is your experience?
- What does it mean to water good seeds?
- Give an example of one instance where you watered a good seed in yourself and others?

For a handout and homework assignments related to lesson four, see pages 196 to 198 in the appendix.

CHAPTER EIGHTEEN

LESSON FIVE: MINDFUL SPEECH AND MAKING HEALTHY DECISIONS

SUFI TRADITION INSTRUCTS us to speak only after our words have passed through four gates. First we must ask if the words we are about to speak are "true," then we must ask if the words are "necessary," then ask if they are "beneficial," and finally ask if the words are "kind." If your words pass through the four gates of "true, necessary, beneficial, and kind," only then can you share them.

In my neighborhood in Delhi I lived within walking distance from the famed Nizamuddin Dargah, a Sufi shrine frequented by persons of all faiths. Every Thursday night the Dargah was packed for the legendary *qawwali*, or devotional Sufi singing. It was here at the Dargah that I learned about the Four Gates of Speech from the Sufi tradition detailed above. Mindful speech is one of the most challenging practices because so much of our society is fueled by gossip and deprecating remarks. By choosing to engage in mindful speech you commit to undoing a lot of cultural conditioning. Professor Gandhi once told me, "Before you speak, think about what you want to create." This is hands-down the best advice I've ever been given. Just as many of us as educators use backward mapping when crafting lessons, imagine how different our lives would be if we also approached life situations with the end in mind. This lesson focuses on how powerful words can be, and it engages students in thinking more deeply about what kind of world they want to create for themselves.

While bringing social emotional learning to young people is incredibly important work, doing it without having the larger conversation around bringing social emotional learning to the systems and structures in which our schools exist is merely putting a Band-Aid on a broken system. My current work focuses on shifting organizational practices in a large urban public school district by making social emotional learning the operating system. It's a challenging task, especially when you have a culture of mistrust fueled by unmindful speech and toxic relationships. If we don't focus on lifting up social emotional learning from the classroom to the boardroom, then this critical work will be seen as just another initiative—bound to eventually fail. I've learned that the way I approach my work must be infused with social emotional learning. Mindful speech and healthy decision making are the most powerful ways of modeling the practice as I strive to build supportive relationships with colleagues around this work of bringing the heart alive in education. As we teach our students the importance of mindful speech, it's vitally important to practice it ourselves in relation to our colleagues and administrators—this is the way our schools will truly transform. Mindfulness at its core is about transformation and liberation from the weight of past mistakes.

Stage One — Desired Results

SUMMARY

The purpose of this lesson is to teach students the importance of mindful speech and strategies for making healthy decisions.

ENDURING UNDERSTANDINGS

Students will understand: Being mindful can help me manage my life more effectively.

ESSENTIAL QUESTIONS

Why be mindful?
What is mindfulness?
How can I be mindful?

KNOWLEDGE CONTENT

Students know:

- The definition of integrity.

SKILLS

Students will be able to:

- Examine how they can make healthy choices.
- Send well-being to others.
- Consider the well-being of a loved one.
- See how our own behavior and choices affect others.
- See the benefit of thinking and considering outcomes before we act.

Stage Two — Assessment Evidence

In each class, students are asked to reflect on the mindfulness practices they are learning by answering orally or in written form the three essential questions: Why be mindful? What is mindfulness? How can I be mindful?

Class discussion about the importance of making healthy decisions relates to students understanding the importance of assuming responsibility for personal health behaviors. Their participation in mindfulness practices demonstrates healthy behaviors.

In this lesson students examine how they make decisions and learn strategies to make healthy choices and apply these strategies to their lives.

Stage Three — Learning Plan

LEARNING ACTIVITIES

Before Class Begins: *Teacher Meditation*

Read and reflect on the following while bringing awareness to your breathing:

> **Truthful and Loving Speech Mindfulness Training:**[34]
> *I am committed to learning to speak truthfully, lovingly, and constructively. I will use only words that inspire joy, confidence, and hope as well as promote reconciliation and peace in myself and among other people. I will speak and listen in a way that can help myself and others transform suffering and see the way out of difficult situations. I am determined not to say untruthful things for the sake of personal interest or to impress people, nor to utter words that might cause division or hatred. I will protect the happiness and harmony of my community by refraining from speaking about the faults of other persons in their absence and always ask myself if my perceptions are correct. I will speak only with the intention to understand and help transform challenging situations. I will not spread rumors nor criticize or condemn things of which I am not sure. I will do my best to speak out about situations of injustice.*

1. Classroom setup

Seating is organized in a circle with desks on the outside. Have gentle music playing.

2. Greet students at the door with your attendance sheet—mindfully take attendance

Make eye contact with each student, smile, welcome them to class, give them any handouts for that day, mark attendance.

3. Being with music

Once the bell rings, invite the bell and have students follow their breath while listening to music. Invite them to follow their breath while remaining aware of the music. Encourage them not to get lost in the music but continue to follow their breath as they listen.

4. Talking Circle—everyone shares reflections from homework using the talking piece

As students share, invite them to also check in with the group around how they are doing emotionally.

5. Making healthy decisions

Share with students that in each moment we have the chance to create a helpful outcome. Ask them what the word "skillful" means to them and guide them toward a shared understanding of how skillful behavior can promote harmony, and how unskillful or unmindful behavior usually doesn't.[35]

Now have them reflect on what integrity means. Also guide them toward a shared understanding. If it feels appropriate, you can offer Oprah's famous quote: "Real integrity is doing the right thing, knowing that nobody's going to know whether you did it or not."

Make sure they understand that when we act in integrity we feel as if we've acted in a way that is in alignment to our beliefs.

6. Reflection

Have students reflect:[36]

- Have you ever acted in a way that may have hurt someone? If so, how did you feel?
- When have you acted with integrity?
- Do you remember not feeling like you acted with integrity? How do you know?

7. How can we make responsible choices?

We are always faced with decisions to make, so how can we make responsible choices?

Ask students how mindfulness may help them make better decisions. Try to remind them about interconnection and interbeing.

Share that some good guidance is to ask yourself: "Could this harm myself or someone else?"[37] If the answer is yes, then it's probably not a good idea to undertake that action.

8. Share the Four Gates of Speech

Sufi tradition instructs us to speak only after our words have passed through four gates. First we must ask if the words we are about to speak are "true," then we must ask if the words are "necessary," then are they "helpful," and finally, are the words "kind." If your words pass through the four gates of "true, necessary, helpful, and kind" then you can share them.

Ask students how different their world would be if everyone practiced the Four Gates of Speech.

9. Needs and Feelings

Ask students about the relationship between feelings and needs. Guide them toward understanding how our feelings have to do with certain needs being met or unmet. For example, you may have a feeling of hunger because you haven't eaten and your need around nourishment hasn't been met, or you may feel connected because your family loves you and your needs around love are being met.

The practice of nonviolent communication (http://www.cnvc.org/) teaches us that needs are behind our feelings. Our feelings result from met or unmet needs.

10. Go over the needs and feelings inventory from the Center for Nonviolent Communication with your students so they get a clear understanding of what needs are

NEEDS[38] (by no means an exhaustive list):

CONNECTION: acceptance, affection, appreciation, belonging, cooperation, communication, closeness, community, companionship, compassion, consideration, consistency, empathy, inclusion, intimacy, love, mutuality, nurturing, respect/self-respect, safety, security, stability, support, to know and be known, to see and be seen, to understand and be understood, trust, warmth; PHYSICAL WELL-BEING: air, food, movement/exercise, rest/sleep, sexual expression, safety, shelter, touch, water; HONESTY: authenticity, integrity, presence; PLAY: joy, humor; PEACE: beauty, communion, ease, equality, harmony, inspiration, order; AUTONOMY: choice, freedom, independence, space, spontaneity; MEANING: awareness, celebration of life, challenge, clarity, competence, consciousness, contribution, creativity, discovery, efficacy, effectiveness, growth, hope, learning, mourning, participation, purpose, self-expression, stimulation, to matter, understanding.

FEELINGS[39] WHEN YOUR NEEDS ARE NOT SATISFIED:
AFRAID: apprehensive, dread, foreboding, frightened, mistrustful, panicked, petrified, scared, suspicious, terrified, wary, worried; **ANGRY:** enraged, furious, incensed, indignant, irate, livid, outraged, resentful; **AVERSION:** animosity, appalled, contempt, disgusted, dislike, hate, horrified, hostile, repulsed; **CONFUSED:** ambivalent, baffled, bewildered, dazed, hesitant, lost, mystified, perplexed, puzzled, torn; **ANNOYED:** aggravated, dismayed, disgruntled, displeased, exasperated, frustrated, impatient, irritated, irked; **DISCONNECTED:** alienated, aloof, apathetic, bored, cold, detached, distant, distracted, indifferent, numb, removed, uninterested, withdrawn; **DISQUIET:** agitated, alarmed, discombobulated, disconcerted, disturbed, perturbed, rattled, restless, shocked, startled, surprised, troubled, turbulent, turmoil, uncomfortable, uneasy, unnerved, unsettled, upset; **EMBARRASSED:** ashamed, chagrined, flustered, guilty, mortified, self-conscious; **FATIGUE:** beat, burnt out, depleted, exhausted, lethargic, listless, sleepy, tired, weary, worn out; **PAIN:** agony, anguished, bereaved, devastated, grief, heartbroken, hurt, lonely, miserable, regretful, remorseful; **SAD:** depressed, dejected, despair, despondent, disappointed, discouraged, disheartened, forlorn, gloomy, heavyhearted, hopeless, melancholy, unhappy; **TENSE:** anxious, cranky, distressed, distraught, edgy, fidgety, frazzled, irritable, jittery, nervous, overwhelmed, restless, stressed out; **VULNERABLE:** fragile, guarded, helpless, insecure, leery, reserved, sensitive, shaky; **YEARNING:** envious, jealous, longing, nostalgic, pining, wistful.

FEELINGS WHEN YOUR NEEDS ARE SATISFIED:

COMPASSION: affectionate, friendly, loving, openhearted, sympathetic, tender, warm; **ENGAGED:** absorbed, alert, curious, engrossed, enchanted, entranced, fascinated, interested, intrigued, involved, spellbound, stimulated; **HOPEFUL:** expectant, encouraged, optimistic; **CONFIDENT:** empowered, open, proud, safe, secure; **EXCITED:** amazed, animated, ardent, aroused, astonished, dazzled, eager, energetic, enthusiastic, giddy, invigorated, lively, passionate, surprised, vibrant. **GRATEFUL:** appreciative, moved, thankful, touched; **INSPIRED:** amazed, awed, wonder; **JOYFUL:** amused, delighted, glad, happy, jubilant, pleased, tickled; **EXHILARATED:** blissful, ecstatic, elated, enthralled, exuberant, rapturous, thrilled; **PEACEFUL:** calm, clearheaded, comfortable, centered, content, equanimous, fulfilled, mellow, quiet, relaxed, relieved, satisfied, serene, still, tranquil, trusting; **REFRESHED:** enlivened, rejuvenated, renewed, rested, restored, revived.

11. With our words we can cause suffering or bring joy. How do you want to speak?

Talk to students about how we are often not aware of how much power lies in our words. Engage them in a discussion about this and focus on the issue of gossip. Share that a great way to check and see if they are gossiping is to reflect on whether they would say the same thing about the person if the person could hear what they are saying.[40]

12. Essential questions

End class by returning to the essential questions: Why be mindful? What is mindfulness? How can I be mindful? Have students reflect on what they learned in this class and connect it to the unit essential questions.

13. Go over homework

Practice looking deeply into your speech. Don't judge yourself, just pay attention to whether your words create happiness or hurt.

Practice the Four Gates of Speech for a few hours before our next class. What did you learn?

For a handout and homework assignments related to lesson five, see pages 199 to 203 in the appendix.

CHAPTER NINETEEN

LESSON SIX: USING TECHNOLOGY MINDFULLY

Time magazine's February 3, 2014 cover story, "The Mindful Revolution," leads with, "Finding peace in a stressed-out, digitally dependent culture may just be a matter of thinking differently."[41] In this lesson, we'll apply the principle of thinking differently, i.e., mindfully, to our tech-saturated lives. In my office, I have a calligraphy of Thich Nhat Hanh's that reads, "Breathe, you are online," and it serves as a constant reminder to come back to my body and recognize—as I mindfully breathe—that I am alive.

Mindfulness has been essential in striking a balance around technology in my life and the irony is that I also use technology to support my mindfulness practice, especially during the workday. From a mindfulness bell that goes off every fifteen minutes on my computer reminding me to breathe, to my cell-phone ringtone, which I also employ as a mindfulness bell (I use the first two rings to breathe and only pick up on the third), I'm harnessing technology to help me maintain presence and practice mindfulness. That being said, my husband and I do our best to set technology limits. We do this to truly come back to ourselves and be fully present for each other. Some of the ways we create boundaries with technology are:

- We intentionally leave our phones at home if we plan on taking a walk, riding bikes, or communing with nature so we can be fully present.
- We have an alarm clock so our cell phones never enter our bedroom, and the time we spend before we sleep and after we wake up are technology free.
- We take technology sabbaticals for at least twenty-four hours one day a week.
- One meal a day is technology free.
- We set fixed times to check email each day depending on our work schedule so we aren't constantly responding to emails throughout the day.

The goal of this lesson is to engage students on how they can use mindfulness to ensure that they control technology and that technology doesn't control them.

Stage One — Desired Results

SUMMARY

The purpose of this lesson is to teach students strategies for using technology mindfully.

ENDURING UNDERSTANDINGS

Students will understand: Being mindful can help me manage my life more effectively.

ESSENTIAL QUESTIONS

Why be mindful?
What is mindfulness?
How can I be mindful?

KNOWLEDGE CONTENT

Students know:

- They have the ability to control technology and not be controlled by it.

SKILLS

Students will be able to:

- Breathe mindfully before picking up the phone, using the "ring" as mindfulness bell.

Stage Two — Assessment Evidence

In each class, students are asked to reflect on the mindfulness practices they are learning by answering orally or in written form the three essential questions: Why be mindful? What is mindfulness? How can I be mindful?

Class discussion about the importance of not being ruled by technology and using it efficiently relates to students understanding the importance of assuming responsibility for personal health behaviors. Their participation in mindfulness practices demonstrates healthy behaviors.

In this lesson students examine how they manage their time with respect to technology and learn strategies like the telephone mindfulness practice to be more efficient and mindful when communicating and using technology.

Stage Three — Learning Plan

LEARNING ACTIVITIES

Before Class Begins: *Teacher Meditation—Tea (or Coffee) Meditation*

While drinking tea, bring awareness to your breathing and silently practice the gatha for drinking tea.[42]

This cup of tea in my two hands—
Mindfulness is held uprightly!
My mind and body dwell
In the very here and now.

1. **Classroom setup**

Organize the seating in a circle with desks on the outside.

2. **Greet students at the door with your attendance sheet—mindfully take attendance**

Make eye contact with each student, smile, welcome them to class, give them any handouts for that day, mark attendance.

3. **Invite the bell, take three breaths as a large group**

4. **Talking Circle—everyone shares reflections from their homework using the talking piece**

Invite students to share how they are doing emotionally.

5. **"Breathe, you are online"**

Ask students what this means.

6. **Mindfulness and technology**

Tell students that today's class is going to focus on strategies to use technology more mindfully. Ask them if their minds are connected to their bodies when they are online.

Now engage them in discussing how they can use technology in a way that enhances their well-being instead of causing stress.

7. You don't need to change what you do; just try and bring awareness to what you are doing

Ask students what happens when they bring mindfulness to any normal activity. Now ask how they think bringing more awareness to their use of technology will affect their experience of it.

Just like situations in life where how we respond and relate is important, the same goes for technology. Ask students how they currently relate to technology. Do they ever check in to what their state of mind is when they are engaging with technology?

8. We are the real power source

Share with students Soren Gordhamer's teaching that they are the "real power source," not the technology itself. "When distraction, fatigue, frustration, or anxiety are engaging, we are like a cell phone without a charge. From this, we can decide what action, if any, to take to increase the power source and to make our time more effective."[43]

Encourage students to first check in with their state of mind when they go online or grab for their phone. If they aren't clear about the state of their mind, have them connect first with their body through mindful stretching or breathing.

9. Whenever you receive a text or email or the phone rings, take the opportunity to first breathe and come back to yourself before you respond

If you practice telephone meditation you can now share with them how the practice has impacted your life. When the phone rings let it be a reminder to be present in your body and with the first two rings practice mindfulness of breathing. Before picking up the phone on the third ring you can silently say to yourself Thich Nhat Hanh's telephone gatha:

Words can travel thousands of miles.
May my words create mutual understanding and love.
May they be as beautiful as gems,
as lovely as flowers.[44]

10. The brain cannot multitask

John Medina's *Brain Rules*, a great resource for exploring the brain with young people, stresses that the brain is not capable of multitasking. "We can talk and breathe, but when it comes to higher level tasks, we just can't do it."[45]

11. Transitional time

Share with students how they can use transitional time to breathe and the statistic that on average we spend three years of our life waiting. Imagine if we used that time breathing mindfully instead of stressing out that we have to wait or are in line!

12. Beginning your day and ending your night with mindfulness

Try and be technology free at least fifteen minutes before you go to bed and fifteen minutes after you get up. Use this time to send yourself metta.

13. Unit essential questions

End class by returning to the unit essential questions: Why be mindful? What is mindfulness? How can I be mindful? Have students reflect on what they learned in this class and connect it to unit essential questions.

14. Homework

Mindful Consumption: We all spend so much time in front of the computer and on our phones. *Reflect on mindful consumption, just like we have the power to choose our language carefully, the experiences we take in also affect us.* Before our next class, pay attention to how your media consumption affects you.

What is your mind like after hours on the Internet, playing video games, social media, or in front of the TV? Detail how you feel.

Try practicing some of the mindfulness strategies we learned in class today like using your telephone ring as a mindfulness bell and breathing in twice before you pick up the phone. What do you experience?

Come up with one of your own mindfulness strategies for using technology.

For handouts and homework with many more activities related to lesson six, see pages 204 to 206 in the appendix.

CHAPTER TWENTY

LESSON SEVEN: PEACE

To me mindfulness is resolving conflicts without getting violent or nasty.
—SOFIA, age 10

One day, before eighth period began, my sixth graders were standing outside my classroom and I could sense something was not right. I went to the door and one of my beautiful students shared, "Everyone is having a bad day." I tuned in to my breath and quickly assessed the situation, paying attention to what the needs might be behind the feelings of my students. One of my boys had said something hurtful about one of my girls in a previous class and she was very, very upset. I looked at all the children and said, "Remember, we are a family in this classroom and we are going to take care of this." I instructed all of the students except the boy and the girl to go inside and get to work on their writing projects with our classroom aide. Instead of calling the counselor, I took the boy and the girl with me to a neighboring room and had them sit down and share how they felt. Before they shared, I had us all breathe, established clear guidelines and then led them through a version of an exercise called Beginning Anew. Beginning anew is a practice developed by the Thich Nhat Hanh community to help manage potential conflict in relationships.

This particular conflict was very emotional. The boy who made the offensive comment was upset that he had hurt his friend and he started crying when she shared how she felt. Initially there was so much anger in the air, I didn't know if beginning anew would be appropriate, but as soon as we got started it became clear to me that the framework of first sharing appreciation, apologizing for unpleasant behavior, sharing our hurt, and asking for support is a very powerful one—it's a framework that promotes authenticity. The whole process in fact took less than ten minutes and we were all able to return to class and be productive. I think it's important as a teacher to address conflict as soon as it arises. Every situation is different and beginning anew may not be the right approach each time, but adapting it can be very helpful in mediating conflict between children.

BEGINNING ANEW

The practice of beginning anew has transformed my close relationships. Finally, I had a framework to help manage conflict and share the difficulties I was having in my relationships with loved ones. The practice consists of four steps and is usually done by both parties, but I've done the practice successfully with myself when I need to "begin anew" and make it optional for students to participate when I share the practice with them during our one-on-one conferences every quarter.

The first part begins with the practice of "watering flowers." It is the idea that in order to keep the flowers of our relationships in bloom, we need to water them with genuine appreciation. We share from our heart the positive qualities we've observed in the other person. We do not share abstract qualities we appreciate in the other person like "kindness" but rather provide concrete examples that demonstrate these qualities such as, "I really appreciated how you came in early before the bell rang and started putting down the chairs for all of your classmates without even being asked. That was very thoughtful." The second step involves sharing our own weaknesses and unskillful actions. With all that happens during the school day, I often seem to be more unskillful than skillful and this step provides me with a space to reflect on specific instances when I've been unskillful and make a commitment to doing better. For example, "I'm sorry that I forgot to change our class jobs this week, and you had to be floor sweeper twice in a row." Depending on the situation, I may stop after the second step, but if I feel it is appropriate then I move on to the third and fourth steps. The first two steps prepare the ground for reconciliation and the third step calls upon us to share how we have been hurt by something we perceive another person has done.

Sharing when we are hurt must be done in a skillful way and it is imperative that we do not blame or judge the other person and simply share what we observed. The fourth step involves asking the other person for support when you are going through a challenging time. When my mom was diagnosed with a degenerative lung disease, I practiced beginning anew with close friends and colleagues and asked for their support, and to this day it is their support that has helped me get through a very challenging time.

In addition to beginning anew, another formal mindfulness practice I've found incredibly helpful for my students and myself in generating a sense of peace both within and with others is called Pebble Meditation. In pebble meditation we use pebbles to help us breathe mindfully and cultivate helpful qualities.

PEBBLE MEDITATION

Pebble meditation is a popular practice in the Plum Village community. Through mindful breathing and visualization, the helpful qualities of freshness, solidity, clarity, and freedom are cultivated using the images of a flower, a mountain, still water, and the spacious blue sky.

When I share the practice with children in the classroom, I sometimes refer to it as "pebble reflection." Some of my students also started calling the activity "peace rocks." At my school in India, the entire fourth grade learns the meditation as part of their social studies unit on peace at the start of the year, and throughout the year pebble meditation is a touchstone practice that they always go back to. In this social studies unit the enduring understanding is "peace in oneself, peace in the world."

Depending on the age of the children I am working with, I introduce one pebble at a time using a worksheet developed in Plum Village that's included in the appendix.

The worksheet and the pebbles help us make what can be abstract concepts into something more concrete. You can also use a plain sheet of paper and fold it into four spaces. As I go through the handout I have children reflect on each image and quality, and choose pebbles to correspond to each image and quality.

The day before I introduce the practice I usually have each of my students bring in four pebbles and I give each of them a small, colorful bag to keep their pebbles. Depending on the age of the students you are working with, you can have them make their own pebble bags. You can also have children decorate their pebbles or even choose their own helpful qualities to cultivate through mindful breathing. I followed the lead of one of my students, Phoebe, who added her very own "love" pebble! When I'm working with middle school or high school students I usually let them choose their own images because it also gives them more ownership with the practice. If you think you may run into some parental concerns regarding visualization, you can alter the wording and instead of seeing oneself as a flower or mountain, you can put more focus on the feeling of freshness or solidity. With younger children I also use this opportunity to teach new vocabulary words like "fresh" and "clarity." This would also be important if you have a lot of English language learners.

For the first pebble, the image is a flower and the quality is freshness. Thich Nhat Hanh often talks about how we are all beautiful flowers in a garden of humanity and when I introduce this pebble I use fresh flowers.

For the second pebble the image is a mountain and the quality we are exploring is solidity. When I introduce this pebble I usually play a game with my students where I also teach them the importance of posture in sitting meditation and we take turns trying to push each other over, and depending on the energy of the class I also may have some students try and push me when I'm seated. When Jon and Myla Kabat-Zinn came to our school, they did the practice with our fourth and fifth graders. After the pebble meditation, Jon asked the children what kinds of weather a mountain might experience. Students shared that a mountain might experience weather that is bright, sunny, foggy, windy, rainy, snowy, etc. Jon then compared the weather to emotions they might feel, helping them see that the weather doesn't keep a mountain from being a mountain. The mountain knows it's solid no matter what is going on around it. He emphasized that the weather is "natural," and we don't have to feel bad about our emotions. Like the weather, emotions are natural and they change quickly. Myla stressed that while introducing the practice it is critical to create a space with children where the whole range of emotions are welcome and accepted. Very often we don't feel fresh, solid, clear, or free, and that's okay. Before we can even think about transformation we have to really ground ourselves in acceptance!

For the third pebble, the image we are working with is still water in a lake, and the quality we are focusing on is clarity. I present the third pebble with a large clear container with water and we

Flower **Fresh**

I feel fresh, energetic, joyful and playful when:

I feel fresh, energetic, joyful and playful when I have just waken up in the morning, and playing with my cat.

Space **Free**

I feel free, light and relaxed when:

I close my eyes and do some breathing.

Mountain **Solid**

I feel solid, strong and confident when: I imagine myself as a mountain strong, solid, ever lasting, slow progeesing. Sometimes coverd by fogs other encased in storms but alway I am a moountain

Rock

Still Water **Reflecting**

I feel calm, still, quiet and focused when:

When I hear the bell in Health

Pebble meditation reflections from Meena's sixth grade students.

first discuss how much of our bodies are made up of water. Then I introduce the word "reflection" and we talk about seeing reflections in lakes. Then I shake the water or have a student shake it and we observe what happens and that is when I may introduce the word "distortion." Usually a child makes a connection between how much water is in our bodies and how when we are "stirred" up, we don't reflect things clearly, and this lends itself to a discussion of how we can make better decisions when we are calm. This pebble helps us calm our body and mind. We all have the capacity for clarity when we touch the still water within.

The image for the fourth pebble is the spacious blue sky, and the quality is freedom, feeling free. When introducing this pebble we talk about what it means to feel free, especially free from worry or anxiety, and I teach the word "spaciousness." Depending on the age of the children I bring in a very small cup and I put a small spoon of salt in it and then I bring in a very large container and put the same amount of salt in it and I share with them one of my favorite Thich Nhat Hanh quotes, "If your cup is small, a little bit of salt will make the water salty. If your heart is small then a little bit of pain will make you suffer. Your heart must be large." In this way we cultivate spaciousness in ourselves. Cultivating spaciousness within helps create the acceptance needed to really practice mindfulness. A great image or visual for this is the sky; you can also talk about the qualities of the sky with the children.

Stage One—Desired Results

SUMMARY

The purpose of this lesson is to teach students practical strategies to help them cultivate peacefulness within so they can be peaceful in the world.

ENDURING UNDERSTANDINGS

Students will understand: Being mindful can help me manage my life more effectively.

ESSENTIAL QUESTIONS

Why be mindful?

What is mindfulness?

How can I be mindful?

KNOWLEDGE CONTENT

Students know:

- Peace is about feeling peaceful and being in a state of harmony. Peace is not about avoiding conflict. We all experience conflict to a greater or lesser degree on a regular basis. The concept of peace has to do with how we deal with conflict.

SKILLS

Students will be able to:

- Practice pebble meditation.
- explore practical methods to resolve conflict such as using a peace treaty or peace note.

Stage Two — Assessment Evidence

In each class, students are asked to reflect on the mindfulness practices they are learning by answering orally or in written form the three essential questions: Why be mindful? What is mindfulness? How can I be mindful?

Class discussion about how stress and conflict relates to students understanding the importance of assuming responsibility for personal health behaviors. Their participation in mindfulness practices demonstrates healthy behaviors to reduce stress and deal with conflict skillfully.

In this lesson students are to examine how they manage and work with stress and conflict and how they can develop peace within. They are given the strategy of the pebble meditation and peace treaty to apply in life.

Stage Three — Learning Plan

LEARNING ACTIVITIES

Before Class Begins: *Teacher Meditation*

Adapted from exercise one from *The Blooming of a Lotus* by Thich Nhat Hanh:[46]

Joy of Meditation as Nourishment

Breathing in, I know I am breathing in. (In)
Breathing out, I know I am breathing out. (Out)

Breathing in, I see myself as a flower. (Flower)
Breathing out, I feel fresh. (Fresh)

Breathing in, I see myself as a mountain. (Mountain)
Breathing out, I feel solid. (Solid)

Breathing in, I see myself as still water. (Still water)
Breathing out, I reflect all that is. (Reflecting)

Breathing in, I see myself as space. (Space)
Breathing out, I feel free. (Free)

1. Classroom setup

Seating is organized in a circle with desks on the outside.

2. Greet students at the door with your attendance sheet—mindfully take attendance

3. Talking Circle: Everyone shares a reflection from their homework using the talking piece

Use this time to also check in with each student about their emotions.

4. "Peace in oneself, peace in the world"

Ask students what this means.

5. What does peace mean to you?

Have students reflect on what peace means to them. Ask them when they are not peaceful and if they have any strategies to "keep the peace" and maintain a sense of peacefulness.

6. Peace strategies

Share with students that today they will learn two strategies to cultivate peace within and with others. Tell them how these strategies have helped you!

7. Pebble meditation

A great resource to support the teaching of this practice is *A Handful of Quiet: Happiness in Four Pebbles* by Thich Nhat Hanh, illustrated by Wietske Vriezen (Parallax Press, 2012).

MATERIALS: mindfulness bell, one sheet of paper folded in fourths, four pebbles for each child, markers, colored pencils, crayons. You can collect the pebbles yourself or have the children collect them.

Have students place their pebbles on their left. Have them connect first with when they feel fresh and draw an image or write a sentence that connects with the image and/or feeling of freshness. Have them continue this for each quality (solidity, clarity, freedom) following the guidelines given in the narrative before the lesson in this chapter.

When they have finished, tell them that they are now going to bring the pebbles to life with these qualities by breathing the qualities into them. Then they can call upon those qualities anytime they take out that pebble to breathe.

Instruct them to sit so that their bellies are not constricted. "Choose which pebble connects most with feeling fresh. Now, place that pebble in your right hand, observe it, and recall when you've felt fresh and gently close your hand as we begin the practice, soften your face, close your eyes."

Wake bell
Breathing in, I see myself as a flower, a human flower.
Breathing out, I am beautiful just as I am and I feel very fresh.
[Breathing in] *flower.*
[Breathing out] *fresh.*
"Breathe three times to the key words *flower/fresh* at your own pace."
Invite the bell (*flower/fresh* three times)
"One of the greatest gifts we can give others is our freshness.

"Now place your flower pebble to your right and pick up your mountain pebble. Take a moment to observe your pebble and recall when you've felt solid and know that that solidity is always with you, no matter what the external circumstances may be. Gently hold your mountain pebble and close your eyes."

Wake bell

Breathing in, I see myself as a mountain.
Breathing out, I feel solid; nothing can move or distract me.
[Breathing in] *mountain.*
[Breathing out] *solid.*
"Breathe three times to the key words *mountain, solid* at your own pace."
Invite bell (*mountain/solid* three times)

"Now place your solid mountain pebble to your right and pick up your still water pebble. Take a look at this pebble and remember that when the water in you is still, you have clarity and can reflect things as they are."

Wake bell

Breathing in, I see myself as still water.
Breathing out, I reflect things as they are with clarity.
[Breathing in] *still water.*
[Breathing out] *I reflect things as they are.*
"Breathe three times to the key phrases *still water, reflecting* at your own pace."
Invite bell (*still water/reflecting* three times)

"Now place your still water reflecting pebble to your right and pick up your space freedom pebble. Take a look at this pebble and remember that when you touch the space you have inside, like the great blue sky you can feel free and not have anxiety or worry."

Wake bell

Breathing in, I see myself as the spacious blue sky.
Breathing out, I feel free, free from anxiety, fear or worry.
[Breathing in] *space.*
[Breathing out] *free.*
"Breathe three times to the key words *space, free* at your own pace."

Invite bell (*space/free* three times)

Invite bell three times to close

OPTIONAL: If you feel it is appropriate with your age group you can teach the song, "Breathing in, Breathing out," written by Thich Nhat Hanh and Betsy Rose.[47]

BREATHING IN, BREATHING OUT

lyrics by Thich Nhat Hanh, music by Betsy Rose

C Am
Breathing in, breathing out . . . *(2x)*
Dm G
I am blooming as a flower.
Dm G7 C
I am fresh as the dew.
Em Am
I am solid as a mountain.
Dm G Am G/B
I am firm as the Earth.
Am G/B C
I am free.

Breathing in, breathing out . . . *(2x)*
I am water reflecting what is real,
what is true.
And I feel there is space deep inside
of me.
C F C
I am free, I am free, I am free.

8. Conflict role play/peace treaty

Invite students to share a time when they were in conflict. Have students act it out and then as a class brainstorm how it could have been handled more skillfully. Help them draw upon all of the strategies they've learned in the unit. Introduce them to "I" statements and practice as a class to take responsibility for feelings without blaming another. For example, I feel ________________when you ________________ because ________________. I know I upset you when I ________________.

You could also introduce the Plum Village practice of the Peace Treaty and Peace Note described in detail on pages 209 to 211, adapting it to fit their needs. Now have the students role play the conflict again, but using the strategies and mindfulness tools they now have.

Go through the peace treaty with students and have them edit it and make changes. Lead a discussion about how they can resolve conflict better with their friends and family.

9. Homework

- Before our next class, practice one pebble from pebble meditation. What did you experience when you practiced pebble meditation?
- Share the peace treaty with one family member. Ask them if both of you can create your own peace treaty to keep harmony in your home.

10. Unit essential questions

End class by returning to the unit essential questions: Why be mindful? What is mindfulness? How can I be mindful? Have students reflect on what they learned in this class and connect it to unit essential questions.

For handouts and homework related to lesson seven, see pages 207 to 212 in the appendix.

CHAPTER TWENTY-ONE

LESSON EIGHT: FINAL REFLECTIONS

SIMON SINEK'S TED TALK "How great leaders inspire action" introduces the concept of the Golden Circle, which identifies answering the why, what, and how in order to have success in an endeavor. When I first came across Sinek's talk, I felt validated, because several years before I'd even heard about the Golden Circle, the essential questions for my mindfulness unit focused on having students answer: Why be mindful? What is mindfulness? How can you be mindful? In every class, we return to these questions with the hope that each lesson expands their answer and that by the final class they can articulate for themselves why one should be mindful, what mindfulness actually is to them, and how they can be mindful. Once students are introduced to mindfulness, continuing to emphasize "why" is critical because it gives the rationale and relevance for mindfulness in their lives.

A mind map, according to author and educational consultant Tony Buzan is "a powerful graphic technique which provides a universal key to unlock the potential of the brain. It harnesses the full range of cortical skills—word, image, number, logic, rhythm, color, and spatial awareness—in a single, uniquely powerful manner. In so doing, it gives you the freedom to roam the infinite expanses of your brain. The mind map can be applied to every aspect of life where improved learning and clearer thinking will enhance human performance."[48]

Mind maps are the perfect culmination to your mindfulness unit as they prompt students to reflect deeply on your unit's essential questions. Mind maps enable them to demonstrate their own understanding of mindfulness in a unique and powerful way. You can then decorate your classroom with their mind maps and refer back to them throughout the year.

Stage One — Desired Results

SUMMARY

The purpose of this lesson is to have students reflect on all of the mindfulness strategies they've learned through creating a mindfulness mind map answering the unit essential questions.

ENDURING UNDERSTANDINGS

Students will understand: Being mindful can help me manage my life more effectively.

ESSENTIAL QUESTIONS

Why be mindful?
What is mindfulness?
How can I be mindful?

KNOWLEDGE CONTENT

Students know:

- Mindfulness is a skill they can employ to work with challenging situations and strong emotions, develop focus and presence, or cultivate peace.

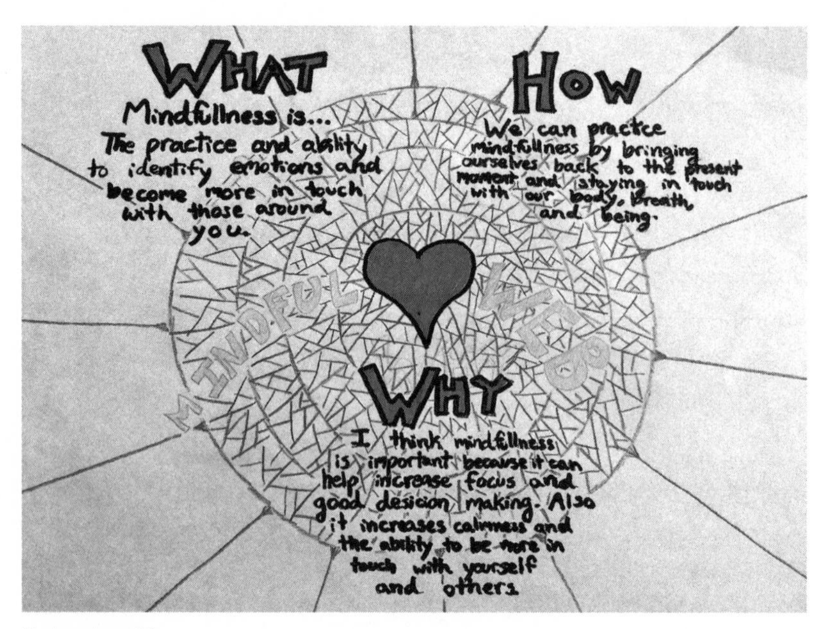

Ruby, Age 12

SKILLS

Students will be able to:

- Recall their most helpful mindfulness strategies.

Stage Two — Assessment Evidence

Students reflect on everything they've learned in the unit and detail their most helpful strategies through answering the unit essential questions (Why be mindful? What is mindfulness? How can I be mindful?) in a mind map that captures their understanding and learning of mindfulness.

Stage Three — Learning Plan

LEARNING ACTIVITIES:

Before Class Begins: *Teacher Meditation*

Bringing awareness to your breathing, silently say to yourself as you breathe:

> *Breathing in, I listen to my students.*
> *Breathing out, I hear what they say.*

1. Classroom setup

Seating is organized in a circle with desks on the outside.

2. Greet students at the door with your attendance sheet—mindfully take attendance

3. Talking Circle: Everyone shares a reflection from their homework using the talking piece

Use this time to also check in with each student about their emotions.

4. Now introduce students to the unit's final assessment: An Essential Questions Mindfulness Mind Map

Tell them they have the rest of the period to work on a mind map that represents their learning of mindfulness and once they are finished we will all share our mind maps with each other in the Talking Circle. Brainstorm the beginnings of a mind map as a class!

Mindfulness Mind Maps

Why is it important to learn to be mindful?
How can I be mindful?
What is mindfulness?

Tony Buzan suggests using the following guidelines for creating mind maps[49]:

- Start in the center with an image of the topic, using at least three colors.
- Use images, symbols, codes, and dimensions throughout your mind map.
- Select key words and print using upper- or lowercase letters.
- Each word/image is best alone and sitting on its own line.
- The lines should be connected, starting from the central image. The central lines are thicker, organic, and flowing, becoming thinner as they radiate out from the center.
- Make the lines the same length as the word/image they support.
- Use multiple colors throughout the mind map, for visual stimulation and also to encode or group.
- Develop your own personal style of mind mapping. (It's been my experience that most students go this route.)
- Use emphasis and show associations in your mind map.

5. Once all students finish, gather them in the Talking Circle and have them each share

6. Assessment

After spending time looking through each child's mind map and looking through your notes from each of their homework assignments and class participation, write a letter from the heart to each student and attach the letter to their unit rubric below.

For handouts and homework related to lesson eight, see page 213 in the appendix.

MINDFULNESS UNIT—RUBRIC FOR ASSESSMENT

This rubric is used to evaluate students at the end of the unit taking into account class participation, how they handle a stressful situation (students are asked to detail how they handle a stressful situation before they are taught mindfulness and after) and their mindfulness journal. Instructors are encouraged to write a personal letter to each student explaining why they received the evaluation they did and draw from notes the instructor has taken after each class, student journals, and the pre/post for the unit. In addition to reading their mindfulness journal after each lesson, it is important for the instructor to reflect on each student in every class to see how they are connecting with the material.

Grade 6–8 National Health Education Standard: Students will demonstrate the ability to practice health-enhancing behaviors and avoid or reduce health risks. As a result of health instruction in grades 6–8, students will:

Benchmarks:

- Demonstrate healthy practices and behaviors that will maintain or improve the health of self and others.
- Explain the importance of assuming responsibility for personal health behaviors.

Grade 6–8 National Health Education Standard: Students will demonstrate the ability to use goal-setting skills to enhance health. As a result of health instruction in grades 6–8, students will:

Benchmarks:

- Assess personal health practices.
- Develop a goal to adopt, maintain, or improve a personal health practice.
- Apply strategies and skills needed to attain a personal health goal.

The rubric below can be used by teachers to assess students understanding and application of mindfulness. The rubric can also be adapted for student self-assessment of mindfulness.

	NOT YET Shows very little understanding of mindfulness. Needs ongoing support.	**BEGINNING** Shows some understanding of mindfulness. Needs regular support.	**DEVELOPING** Shows understanding of mindfulness. Needs some support.	**SECURE** Consistently understands and applies mindfulness independently.
ENDURING UNDERSTANDING Mindfulness is a skill I can cultivate to help me manage my life more effectively.				

Idan, age 11

Camille, age 11

AFTERWORD

Vulnerability sounds like truth and feels like courage.
—BRENE BROWN

I STILL EXPERIENCE moments of stress, strong emotions, fear, and pain, but now I have the tools to work with my suffering. Mindfulness helps me embrace vulnerability so I can try to build the authentic relationships that are so central to teaching young people and adults. After a decade of classroom teaching I'm now trying to navigate the world of bringing social emotional learning to more than 40,000 students, teachers, and leaders in a large, urban public school district.

On October 2, the anniversary of Mahatma Gandhi's birthday, I accompanied thousands of others in a walk for peace from Vijay Chowk outside of Parliament to the grand monument of India Gate in the very heart of Delhi. In honor of Gandhi, the peace walk was an expression of nonviolent action in response to several bombings that had shaken the city in the past month. As we walked in silence trying to cultivate peace within ourselves so that we can be peaceful in the outer world, I felt a deep sense of hope despite all of the bloodshed and violence my adopted city had faced. Even today in Oakland, where shootings seem to happen weekly, that same hope remains within me. Hope, as the late Vaclav Havel reminds us, is "definitely not the same thing as optimism. It is not the conviction that something will turn out well, but the certainty that something makes sense, regardless of how it turns out." I am certain that mindfulness makes sense. Through mindfulness we cultivate intimacy with ourselves and others—this has the potential to build a more connected, collaborative, creative society.

Mindfulness is not a universal remedy for poverty, racism, or mental illness, but it is a tool that can help us all build more understanding so we can approach our work as educators with integrity, equity, and compassion. Some of the guiding principles for our social emotional learning work in our district are acceptance, inquiry, and "be the change you want to be." All of these principles are deeply rooted in mindful practice. Just as we accept how we are feeling and what's happening inside us in the moment, we also accept where we are in our practice, and in moving our work forward in the district, and we do this without judgment. Once we accept what we are feeling and where we are, we then engage in inquiry so we can build greater understanding inside and outside ourselves. Humble inquiry, "the fine art of drawing someone out, of asking questions to which you do not know the answer, of building a relationship based on curiosity and interest in the other person,"[50] is how we go about our district work. Through engaging with others from a stance of humble inquiry, we model how to change the way work is done in our district. Transformation begins with oneself and through "being the change," we strive to embody the social emotional skills needed to help make our world a better place.

Mindfulness can enhance students' academic and social and emotional learning as well as teachers' professional performance and job satisfaction. But mindfulness is so much more than providing teachers and their students with tools to increase their resilience and reduce and manage stress; ultimately, mindfulness is about walking the path of awakening, and trying to see the lesson in every breath. The path is, in fact, limitless. While I continue to have my share of unmindful moments every day, I know I'm okay as long as I continue to practice with an open heart. May we all teach, breathe, and learn together.

APPENDIX

MINDFULNESS AS A LEARNED SKILL CURRICULUM:

HANDOUTS AND HOMEWORK

LESSON ONE
INTRODUCTION AND BEING PRESENT THROUGH BREATH AWARENESS

STUDENT HANDOUT

Sometimes your joy is the source of your smile, but sometimes your smile can be the source of your joy.

—THICH NHAT HANH

- Golden Rule—Treat others as you would like to be treated.
- Mindfulness is a skill that can help us be in the present.
- Benefits of Practicing Mindfulness
  - Maintain/focus attention
  - Work skillfully with our emotions
  - Manage stress
  - Develop a sense of inner peace
  - Promote compassion and kindness toward oneself and others
  - Be resilient; recognize interdependence/ interconnection
  - Foster understanding
  - Communicate effectively
  - Make healthy decisions
- Mindfulness and the Brain
  - Hebb's Rule: "Neurons that fire together, wire together."
  - The more we practice mindfulness, just like any other skill, we can improve our ability to focus, be

more aware, and gain understanding of ourselves and others.

- AIE—Attitude Is Everything!

PAYING ATTENTION EXERCISE

Focus on the still object placed in the center of the circle for thirty seconds and fill out the chart below. Place a mark in each section when your mind wanders away from the present moment.

PAST	FUTURE

What did you discover from this exercise about paying attention?

The breath is your best friend!

The most effective way we can bring our mind back to the present moment is by paying attention to our breath.

We can't breathe in the future or the past, only in the present.

Belly Breathing

Inhale

Breathe in = belly big

Exhale

Breathe out = belly small

You should know how to breathe, in order to maintain mindfulness!

LESSON ONE
INTRODUCTION AND BEING PRESENT THROUGH BREATH AWARENESS

HOMEWORK

BEING PRESENT THROUGH BREATH AWARENESS

Breathe mindfully for one minute and then focus on a still object for thirty seconds and see if there is any difference in your concentration from when you did the exercise in class. Write your answers below.

Strategies for helping your attention stay with your breathing:

- Explore the sensations of breathing. Just focus on how you feel when you breathe.
- Quietly say in your head, "in" while you breathe in and "out" while you breathe out.
- Count your breaths to ten.

PAYING ATTENTION EXERCISE

Breathe mindfully for one minute and then focus on a still object for thirty seconds. Fill in the chart below if your mind wanders just like you did in class.

PAST	FUTURE

Answer this question: Was there any difference in your concentration after you spent one minute breathing compared to when you did the exercise in class?

Answer the essential questions in at least one or two sentences. There is NO right or wrong answer!

Why be mindful?

What is mindfulness?

How can you be mindful?

LESSON TWO
BEING PRESENT THROUGH BODY AWARENESS

STUDENT HANDOUT

This is where you will complete your in-class reflections and homework.

MINDFUL WALKING

Take a few deep breaths and try to commit to just being aware of the sensations you experience as you walk, your internal state (feelings, thoughts, etc.), and your outer environment (what you see, smell, feel, etc.).

You can walk mindfully anywhere! As you begin, first bring your attention to the sensation of your feet touching the floor/ground. What does the process of moving your legs feel like? What muscles do you use?

Now try to hold your awareness on your surroundings. Take in the smells, sounds, and feelings. Do you feel a breeze? Does the air smell fresh? Are birds chirping? What do you see around you?

Maintain your focus on the sensation of walking and your surrounding environment. If possible, also get attuned to your internal state—your thoughts and feelings. If you notice your attention moving away from the experience of walking itself and getting lost in thought, gently bring yourself back. It's hard to maintain focus, but each time you practice your focus gets stronger.

LESSON TWO
BEING PRESENT THROUGH BODY AWARENESS

HOMEWORK

1. **Practice gatha walking** for at least thirty steps. Remember to choose a positive word and coordinate each step with your breath and that word, just like we did in class. Write your response below:

How did you feel before gatha walking?

What was your gatha?

How did you feel after gatha walking?

2. **Deep relaxation**

Have a parent or friend read the script below slowly and take a few breaths after each sentence so you can create a comfortable pace for the deep relaxation.

> Take some time now to get very comfortable on your back.
>
> Congratulate yourself because you are now taking some very important time just for you to relax. This is time we rarely spend in our busy

lives. Once you are in a comfortable position, gently close your eyes and, if you can, bring a half smile to your face. Now bring awareness to your breathing. If it is helpful you can place one hand on your chest and one on your belly and you can feel your belly and chest rise and fall as you breathe. With each breath in and out silently count to yourself, *One, two, three . . .*

As you breathe, feel your body on the floor and sink deep into the ground: You are safe; you are protected. Inhaling and exhaling, inhaling and exhaling, you relax your whole body, relax your whole body. Breathing in and breathing out, your whole body feels weightless, as if you are floating on the water or a fluffy cloud.

You have nowhere to be but right here, relaxing with your breath, no worries, no tension, just breathing in and breathing out.

Breathing in, bring awareness to your arms. Breathing out, release any tension you may have in your arms all the way down to your hands. Breathing in bring awareness to your hands, breathing out focus on your right hand. As you breathe bring your awareness to each finger—thumb, index finger, middle finger, ring finger, pinky. Breathing in, focus on the palm of your right hand; breathing out, relax your entire hand. Now bring awareness to your left hand. Breathing in focus on each finger—thumb, index finger, middle finger, ring finger, pinky. Breathing in focus on the palm of your left hand, breathing out relax your entire hand. Now breathe deeply and send love and gratitude to both of your hands. Our hands make it possible for us to draw, play sports, cook, and so much more. Our hands are very precious.

Breathing in, bring your awareness to your legs. Breathing out, relax your legs completely. As you move your awareness down your right leg release any tension you may feel from your thighs to your knees to your calves, to your ankles and finally to your right foot. Breathing in and out, big toe, second toe, middle toe, fourth toe, pinky toe. Breathing in bring awareness to your left leg. Breathing out, as you move your awareness down your left right leg release any tension you may feel from your thighs to your knees to your calves, to your ankles and finally to your left foot. Now bring awareness to each toe on your left foot. Breathing in and out, big toe, second toe, middle toe, fourth toe, pinky toe. Wiggle your toes as you release and relax your feet. Our feet bring us so much joy; they make it possible to skip, play soccer, and dance. Send love and gratitude to your feet.

Now move up your body to the top of your head. Breathing in and out release any tension you may have in your forehead. Take a few breaths as you relax the muscles around your head and feel the weight of your head on the ground. Now, breathing in, bring awareness to your eyes, allow your eyes to completely relax, and breathing out, release any tension you may have around your eyes. Our eyes bring so much beauty to sight, we are so grateful for our eyes. Now send love to your eyes and let them rest.

Breathing in, bring your awareness to your mouth. Breathing out, allow your mouth to relax. Release any tension you have around your mouth. Perhaps you still have that gentle half smile on your face, did you know that smiling releases the tension in the hundreds of muscles in your face? Feel the tension release as you smile. Our mouths enable us to eat, sing, and take in fresh air. Send love and thanks to your mouth.

Now breathing in, bring your awareness to your shoulders. Breathing out, allow your shoulders to completely release and relax. Let all the tension in your shoulders release into the floor and exit your body. Breathing in, send care to your shoulders; breathing out, send your shoulders love.

Breathing in, bring your awareness to your heart. Breathing out, allow your heart to relax. Our hearts works so hard 24/7 but we forget to recognize our hearts and send them love. With each breath embrace your heart with kindness, gratitude, and love. Silently thank your heart for all it does to keep you alive.

[Play relaxing music for some minutes.]

Bring your awareness back to your breathing . . . to your belly rising and falling. Following your breathing, become aware of your arms and legs. You can now stretch if you'd like, and when you feel ready, slowly sit up. You can stretch more, and, when you feel ready, slowly and mindfully stand up.

How did you feel before deep relaxation?

How did you feel during deep relaxation?

How did you feel after deep relaxation?

LESSON THREE
INTERCONNECTION, KINDNESS, AND GRATITUDE

STUDENT HANDOUT

This is where you will complete your in-class reflections and homework.

SMILING STRATEGY

Write down your experience:

MINDFUL EATING

What was the difference between eating the food item normally compared to mindfully?

KINDNESS

Define kindness:

GRATITUDE

Define gratitude:

Brainstorm for your "Gratitude Card."

LESSON THREE
INTERCONNECTION, KINDNESS, AND GRATITUDE

HOMEWORK

1. **Practice the smiling strategy**

What did you discover after practicing this strategy?

What do you think about this quote? "Sometimes your joy is the source of your smile, but sometimes your smile can be the source of your joy." —Thich Nhat Hanh

2. **Mindfully eat one food item**

Eating mindfully is about the quality of living in the moment. Breathe in and out three times before you eat. Look closely at your food and smell it. Place the food in your mouth without chewing it. How does it taste and feel? Pay attention to the experience of chewing and swallowing. Eat slowly. Think about "Interbeing" and the food contemplations.

What did you eat mindfully?

What did you experience?

What does it mean to savor something?

You were introduced to food contemplations in class; now come up with your own that you can say before you eat!

3. Gratitude

Reflect on what you are grateful for each night before you go to bed:

Does the strategy of "reflecting on what you are grateful for" work to make you feel happy?

LESSON FOUR
WORKING WITH EMOTIONS AND WATERING HELPFUL SEEDS

STUDENT HANDOUT

This is where you will complete your in-class notes.

What are emotions? (Write down the definitions you came up with as a class.)

Steps for working with emotions: BCOOL

Breathe: Take three deep breaths. Your breath helps you create awareness of what is happening in the here and now.

Calm: Your breath can also help you calm yourself.

Okay: Once you calm yourself down you'll know that you are ultimately okay and that whatever you are facing is workable. We need to be able to accept whatever we are experiencing.

Observe: Once you feel better you can observe the emotion while it is happening. Naming the emotion can help it feel less overwhelming. "I'm feeling anger right now." Whatever the emotion is try to experience it fully, don't judge it, there's nothing wrong with it. Once you have labeled and accepted the emotion as it is ask yourself, "What do I feel in my body?" "Why is this emotion there?"

Love: Using your breath, hold yourself with love. Be kind to yourself when you experience a challenging emotion. If it is still too overwhelming, try to turn your attention to your breath. You are not trying to ignore your emotion; you are trying to see it clearly. Through clearly seeing your emotion you will take it less personally.

WATERING HELPFUL SEEDS

Inside we have all kinds of seeds. All the time we are watering seeds, but we can build mindfulness and try to water the helpful seeds in ourselves and others more than the unhelpful seeds.

Mindfulness helps us become aware of what seeds we are watering!

LESSON FOUR
WORKING WITH EMOTIONS AND WATERING HELPFUL SEEDS

HOMEWORK

EMOTIONS

Observe yourself closely before our next class and reflect on the ways in which you work with emotions. Do you react to them? Suppress them?

Next time a strong emotion comes up, practice BCOOL. What is your experience?

What does it mean to water good seeds?

Give an example of one instance where you watered a good seed in yourself and others.

LESSON FIVE
MINDFUL SPEECH AND MAKING HEALTHY DECISIONS

STUDENT HANDOUT

> Real integrity is doing the right thing, knowing that nobody's going to know whether you did it or not.
>
> —OPRAH

In each moment we have the chance to create a helpful outcome. Skillful behavior can promote harmony and unskillful or unmindful behavior usually doesn't.[51]

What does integrity mean?

REFLECTIONS

Have you ever acted in a way that may have hurt someone? If so, how did you feel?[52]

When have you acted with integrity?[53]

Do you remember feeling like you didn't act with integrity? How do you know?[54]

THE FOUR GATES OF SPEECH

Sufi tradition instructs us to speak only after our words have passed through four gates. First we must ask if the words we are about to speak are "true," then we must ask if the words are "necessary," then are they, "beneficial," and finally, are the words "kind." If your words pass through the four gates of "true, necessary, beneficial, and kind," then you can share them.

Ask students how different their world would be if everyone practiced the four gates of speech.

Gossip: To check and see if you are gossiping, reflect on whether you would say the same thing if the person you are talking about could hear what you say. If you wouldn't, then it's gossip.[55]

NEEDS AND FEELINGS (NONVIOLENT COMMUNICATION)

The practice of nonviolent communication teaches us that needs are behind our feelings. Our feelings result from met or unmet needs.

NEEDS[56] (by no means an exhaustive list):

CONNECTION: acceptance, affection, appreciation, belonging, cooperation, communication, closeness, community, companionship, compassion, consideration, consistency, empathy, inclusion, intimacy, love, mutuality, nurturing, respect/self-respect, safety, security, stability, support, to know and be known, to see and be seen, to understand and be understood, trust, warmth; PHYSICAL WELL-BEING: air, food, movement/exercise, rest/sleep, sexual expression, safety, shelter, touch, water; HONESTY: authenticity, integrity, presence; PLAY: joy, humor; PEACE: beauty, communion, ease, equality, harmony, inspiration, order; AUTONOMY: choice, freedom, independence, space, spontaneity; MEANING: awareness, celebration of life, challenge, clarity, competence, consciousness, contribution, creativity, discovery, efficacy, effectiveness, growth, hope, learning, mourning, participation, purpose, self-expression, stimulation, to matter, understanding.

FEELINGS[57] WHEN YOUR NEEDS ARE NOT SATISFIED:

AFRAID: apprehensive, dread, foreboding, frightened, mistrustful, panicked, petrified, scared, suspicious, terrified, wary, worried; ANNOYED: aggravated, dismayed, disgruntled, displeased, exasperated, frustrated, impatient, irritated, irked; ANGRY: enraged, furious, incensed, indignant, irate, livid, outraged, resentful; AVERSION: animosity, appalled, contempt, disgusted, dislike, hate, horrified, hostile, repulsed; CONFUSED: ambivalent, baffled, bewildered, dazed, hesitant, lost, mystified, perplexed, puzzled, torn; DISCONNECTED: alienated, aloof, apathetic, bored, cold, detached, distant, distracted, indifferent, numb, removed, uninterested, withdrawn; DISQUIET: agitated, alarmed, discombobulated, disconcerted, disturbed, perturbed, rattled, restless, shocked, startled, surprised, troubled, turbulent, turmoil, uncomfortable, uneasy, unnerved, unsettled, upset; EMBARRASSED: ashamed, chagrined, flustered, guilty, mortified, self-conscious; FATIGUE: beat, burnt out, depleted, exhausted, lethargic, listless, sleepy, tired, weary, worn out; PAIN: agony, anguished, bereaved, devastated, grief, heartbroken, hurt, lonely, miserable, regretful, remorseful; SAD: depressed, dejected, despair, despondent, disappointed, discouraged, disheartened, forlorn, gloomy, heavyhearted, hopeless, melancholy, unhappy; TENSE: anxious, cranky, distressed, distraught, edgy, fidgety, frazzled, irritable, jittery, nervous, overwhelmed, restless, stressed out; VULNERABLE: fragile, guarded, helpless, insecure, leery, reserved, sensitive, shaky; **YEARNING**: envious, jealous, longing, nostalgic, pining, wistful.

FEELINGS WHEN YOUR NEEDS ARE SATISFIED:

COMPASSION: affectionate, friendly, loving, openhearted, sympathetic, tender, warm; **ENGAGED**: absorbed, alert, curious, engrossed, enchanted, entranced, fascinated, interested, intrigued, involved, spellbound, stimulated; **HOPEFUL**: expectant, encouraged, optimistic; **CONFIDENT**: empowered, open, proud, safe, secure; **EXCITED**: amazed, animated, ardent, aroused, astonished, dazzled, eager, energetic, enthusiastic, giddy, invigorated, lively, passionate, surprised, vibrant. **GRATEFUL**: appreciative, moved, thankful, touched; **INSPIRED**: amazed, awed, wonder; **JOYFUL**: amused, delighted, glad, happy, jubilant, pleased, tickled; **EXHILARATED**: blissful, ecstatic, elated, enthralled, exuberant, rapturous, thrilled; **PEACEFUL**: calm, clearheaded, comfortable, centered, content, equanimous, fulfilled, mellow, quiet, relaxed, relieved, satisfied, serene, still, tranquil, trusting; **REFRESHED**: enlivened, rejuvenated, renewed, rested, restored, revived.

LESSON FIVE
MINDFUL SPEECH AND MAKING HEALTHY DECISIONS

HOMEWORK

1. **Practice looking deeply into your speech.** Don't judge yourself, just pay attention to whether your words create happiness or hurt.

What did you discover?

2. **Practice the Four Gates of Speech for a few hours before our next class.**

What did you learn?

LESSON SIX
USING TECHNOLOGY MINDFULLY

STUDENT HANDOUT

This is where you will complete your in-class reflections and homework.

What does "Breathe, you are online?" mean?

What happens when you bring awareness to what you are doing?

What does it mean to be the real power source?[58]

Whenever you receive a text or email or the phone rings take the opportunity to first breathe and come back to yourself before you respond.

Thich Nhat Hanh's telephone gatha

Words can travel thousands of miles.
May my words create mutual understanding and love.
May they be as beautiful as gems, as lovely as flowers.

What are your thoughts on multitasking?

Transitional Time: On average we spend three years of our life waiting. Imagine if we used that time breathing mindfully instead of stressing out that we have to wait or are in line!

Beginning your day and ending your night with mindfulness: Try and be technology free at least fifteen minutes before you go to bed and fifteen minutes after you get up. Use this time to send yourself metta.

LESSON SIX
USING TECHNOLOGY MINDFULLY

HOMEWORK

MINDFUL CONSUMPTION

We all spend so much time in front of the computer and on our phones. Reflect on mindful consumption. Just like we have the power to choose our language carefully, the experiences we take in also affect us. Before our next class pay attention to how your consumption affects you.

What is your mind like after hours on the Internet, playing video games, social media, or in front of the TV? Detail how you feel.

Try practicing some of the mindfulness strategies we learned in class today like using your telephone ring as a mindfulness bell and breathing in twice before you pick up the phone. What do you experience?

Come up with one of your own mindfulness strategies for using technology.

LESSON SEVEN
PEACE

STUDENT HANDOUT

PEACE STRATEGIES

Peace in Me

Pebble Meditation: Keep your pebbles with you and whenever you feel stressed or non-peaceful you can reach for the pebble you need and breathe!

To practice pebble meditation find a quiet spot, get comfortable, and make sure you can breathe deeply out of your belly. Close your eyes if you feel safe enough and if not, half close them. Become aware of your breathing and as you hold each pebble, say the key word silently to yourself for the in-breath and then the out-breath. Breathe slowly and deeply, staying relaxed. Do this three times for each pebble.

Peace with Others

Peace Note: This note can be used with the peace treaty. You can copy it and keep blank copies available in your home and use it whenever you need it.

Peace Treaty[73]*:* How can you deal with conflict better?

PEBBLE REFLECTION PRACTICE SHEET[72]

Finish each sentence and/or draw a picture.

Flower | Fresh

I feel fresh, energetic, joyful, and playful when:

Mountain | Solid

I feel solid, strong, and confident when:

Still Water | Reflecting

I feel calm, still, quiet, and focused when:

Space | Free

I feel free, light, and relaxed when:

This practice sheet was developed by the Plum Village Mindfulness Practice Center.

PEACE NOTE

Date:

Time:

Dear ____________________________,

This morning (afternoon), you said (did) something that made me very angry. I suffered very much. I want you to know this. You said (did):

Please let us both look at what you said (did) and examine the matter together in a calm and open manner this Friday evening.

Yours, not very happy right now,
[your name]

This Peace Note has been adapted from Touching Peace *by Thich Nhat Hanh (Parallax Press, 1994).*

PEACE TREATY

In order that we live happily together and deepen our love and understanding for each other, we the undersigned, commit to observing and practicing the following:

I, the one who is angry, agree to:

1. Refrain from saying or doing anything that might cause further damage or escalate the anger.
2. Not suppress my anger.
3. Practice breathing.
4. Calmly, within twenty-four hours, tell the one who has made me angry about my anger and suffering, either verbally or by delivering a Peace Note.
5. Ask for an appointment for later in the week (e.g., Friday evening) to discuss this matter more thoroughly, either verbally or by peace note.
6. Not say: "I am not angry. It's okay. I am not suffering. There is nothing to be angry about, at least not enough to make me angry."
7. Practice breathing and looking deeply into my daily life—while sitting, lying down, standing, and walking—in order to see:
    a. the ways I myself have been unskillful at times.
    b. how I have hurt the other person
    c. how the strong seed of anger in me is the primary cause of my anger.
    d. how the other person's suffering, which waters the seed of my anger, is the secondary cause.
    e. how the other person is only seeking relief from his or her own suffering.
    f. that as long as the other person suffers, I cannot be truly happy.
8. Apologize immediately, without waiting until the Friday evening, as soon as I realize my unskillfulness and lack of mindfulness.

9. Postpone the Friday meeting if I do not feel calm enough to meet with the other person.

I, the one who has made the other angry, agree to:

1. Respect the other person's feelings, not ridicule him or her, and allow enough time for him or her to calm down.
2. Not press for an immediate discussion.
3. Confirm the other person's request for a meeting, either verbally or by note, and assure him or her that I will be there.
4. Practice breathing to see how:
   - a. I have seeds of unkindness and anger to make the other person unhappy.
   - b. I have mistakenly thought that making the other person suffer would relieve my own suffering.
   - c. by making him or her suffer, I make myself suffer.
5. Apologize as soon as I realize my unskillfulness and lack of mindfulness, without making any attempt to justify myself and without waiting until the Friday meeting.

We vow with Earth as witness and the supportive presence of our community, to abide by these guidelines.

Signed,
[name]

the ________Day of ____________________in the Year ________ at (location)____________________.

This Peace Treaty has been adapted from Touching Peace *by Thich Nhat Hanh (Parallax Press, 1994).*

LESSON SEVEN
PEACE

HOMEWORK

Before our next class, practice one pebble from pebble meditation.

What did you experience when you practiced pebble meditation?

LESSON EIGHT
FINAL REFLECTIONS: MINDFULNESS MIND MAPS

HANDOUT

Your homework is to complete your mind map and answer each of these questions below. Each leg of your mind map should relate to each question.

Why is it important to learn to be mindful?

How can I be mindful?

What is mindfulness?

Your mindfulness mind map is your final assessment for this unit.

NOTES

1 Haim G. Ginott, *Teacher and Child: A Book for Parents and Teachers* (New York: Collier Books, 1993).

2 Parker J. Palmer, *The Courage to Teach: Exploring the Inner Landscape of a Teacher's Life* (San Francisco: Jossey-Bass, 1998).

3 Parker J. Palmer, *Let Your Life Speak: Listening for the Voice of Vocation* (San Francisco: Jossey-Bass, 2000).

4 Meiklejohn et al., "Integrating Mindfulness Training into K–12 Education: Fostering the Resilience of Teachers and Students," *Mindfulness*, Springer 2012: 1–2.

5 Palmer, *The Courage to Teach.*

6 Plum Village, "Contemplations Before Eating." http://plumvillage.org/news/contemplations-before-eating.

7 Soren Gordhamer, *Wisdom 2.0: Ancient Secrets for the Creative and Constantly Connected* (New York: HarperOne, 2008).

8 Salzberg, Sharon. "Relearning Loveliness." *Lovingkindness: The Revolutionary Art of Happiness.* Boston: Shambhala, 1995. 28.

9 Charles Osborne, *W. H. Auden: The Life of a Poet* (London: Methuen, 1980).

10 Robert A. Emmons, *Thanks!: How the New Science of Gratitude Can Make You Happier* (Boston: Houghton Mifflin, 2007).

11 Thich Nhat Hanh, *The Heart of Understanding: Commentaries on the Prajñaparamita Heart Sutra* (Berkeley, CA: Parallax Press, 1988).

12 Center for Courage and Renewal, "Circle of Trust Touchstones" in *Center for Courage and Renewal Circle of Trust Touchstones* (2012) http://www.couragerenewal.org/images/stories/Touchstones-CCR-rev9-12.pdf.

13 Thich Nhat Hanh, *The Blooming of a Lotus: Guided Meditation Exercises for Healing and Transformation* (Boston: Beacon Press, 1993).

14 Thich Nhat Hanh, *Mindful Movements: Ten Exercises for Well-Being* (Berkeley, CA: Parallax Press, 2008).

15 National School Reform Faculty, "Consultancy Protocol Overview," (Harmony Education Center, 2014).

16 Grant P. Wiggins and Jay McTighe, *Understanding by Design*, expanded 2nd ed. (Alexandria, VA: Association for Supervision and Curriculum Development, 2005).

17 CASEL, "SEL Core Competencies," (CASEL, www.casel.org).

18 Center for Investigating Healthy Minds, "Welcome to the Center for Investigating Healthy Minds" (University of Wisconsin–Madison, n.d., http://www.investigatinghealthyminds.org).

19 Caring School Community, "Teacher Facilitation Techniques." Developmental Studies Center, n.p., n.d. (http://www.devstu.org/blogs/engaging-the-disengaged-number-six).

20 CASEL, "CASEL | Definition," http://www.casel.org/basics/definition.php.

21 American Cancer Society, *National Health Education Standards Achieving Excellence,* 2nd ed. (Atlanta, GA: American Cancer Society, 2007).

22 Harry K. Wong and Rosemary T. Wong, *The First Days of School: How to Be an Effective Teacher,* 2nd ed. (Mountain View, CA: Harry K. Wong Publications, 1998).

23 Nicholas Yoder, "Teaching the Whole Child Instructional Practices That Support Social-Emotional Learning in Three Teacher Evaluation Frameworks," *Research to Practice Brief* Center on Great Teachers and Leaders at American Institutes for Research, n.d.), http://www.gtlcenter.org/sites/default/file.

24 Oakland Unified School District, "Restorative Justice," *Learn More About* (Oakland, CA, 2012), http://www.ousd.k12.ca.us/Page/1052.

25 Thich Nhat Hanh, *The Blooming of a Lotus.*

26 Mindfulnet.org, "Mindfulness in Schools: Learning Lessons from the Adults, Secular and Buddhist," www.mindfulnet.org, http://www.mindfulnet.org/Mindfulness_in_Schools_Burnett_2009.pdf.

27 Adherents.com, "The Religion of Phil Jackson, Basketball Coach," http://www.adherents.com/people/pj/Phil_Jackson.html.

28 Thich Nhat Hanh, *The Blooming of a Lotus.*

29 Thich Nhat Hanh, *Mindful Movements.*

30 Thich Nhat Hanh, *The Blooming of a Lotus.*

31 Thich Nhat Hanh, *The Heart of Understanding.*

32 Associated Press, "Metta World Peace: Ron Artest changes name to better the world," *The Christian Science Monitor,* http://www.csmonitor.com/The-Culture/Latest-News-Wires/2011/0917/Metta-World-Peace-Ron-Artest-changes-name-to-better-the-world.

33 Thich Nhat Hanh, *The Blooming of a Lotus.*

34 Order of Interbeing, "Order of Interbeing | Tiep Hien," http://www.orderofinterbeing.org/for-the-aspirant/fourteen-mindfulness-trainings/.

35 Diana Winston, *Wide Awake: A Buddhist Guide for Teens* (New York: Perigee Book, 2003).

36 Winston, *Wide Awake.*

37 Winston, *Wide Awake.*

38 Center for Nonviolent Communication, "Center for Nonviolent Communication Needs Inventory," http://www.cnvc.org/Training/needs-inventory.

39 Center for Nonviolent Communication "Center for Nonviolent Communication Feelings Inventory," https://www.cnvc.org/Training/feelings-inventory.

40 Winston, *Wide Awake.*

41 Kate Pickert, "The Mindful Revolution," *Time* (Time Inc., Feb. 2, 2014), http://time.com/1556/the-mindful-revolution/.

42 Thich Nhat Hanh, "Thich Nhat Hanh's Gathas," *Here and Now,* n.p. n.d., http://mindfulgatha.wordpress.com/gathas/.

43 Gordhamer, *Wisdom 2.0.*

44 Thich Nhat Hanh, *The Miracle of Mindfulness: An Introduction to the Practice of Meditation*, unabridged ed. (Boston, MA: Beacon Press, 2014).

45 BrainRules.net, "Attention | Brain Rules," n.d., http://www.brainrules.net/attention.

46 Thich Nhat Hanh, *The Blooming of a Lotus.*

47 Betsy Rose, and Thich Nhat Hanh, "Breathing In, Breathing Out" in Thich Nhat Hanh, *Planting Seeds: Practicing Mindfulness with Children* (Berkeley, CA: Parallax Press, 2013).

48 Tony Buzan, "Mind Mapping," n.p., n.d., http://www.tonybuzan.com/about/mind-mapping/.

49 Ibid.

50 Schein, Edgar H. *Helping: How to Offer, Give, and Receive Help.* (San Francisco: Berrett-Koehler Publishers, 2009).

51 Winston, *Wide Awake.*

52 Winston, *Wide Awake.*

53 Winston, *Wide Awake.*

54 Winston, *Wide Awake.*

55 Winston, *Wide Awake.*

56 Winston, *Wide Awake*.

57 Kate Pickert, "The Mindful Revolution," *Time* (Time Inc., Feb. 2, 2014), http://time.com/1556/the-mindful-revolution/.

58 Gordhamer, *Wisdom 2.0*.

RECOMMENDED RESOURCES

Reading

Amstutz, Lorraine Stutzman, and Judy H. Mullet. *The Little Book of Restorative Discipline for Schools: Teaching Responsibility, Creating Caring Climates.* Intercourse, PA: Good Books, 2005.

Nhat Hanh, Thich. *Being Peace.* Berkeley, CA: Parallax Press, 2005.

———. *How to Sit.* Berkeley, CA: Parallax Press, 2014.

———. *The Miracle of Mindfulness: A Manual on Meditation.* Rev. ed. Boston: Beacon Press, 1987.

———. *Present Moment Wonderful Moment: Mindfulness Verses for Daily Living.* Berkeley, CA: Parallax Press, 1993.

Hanson, Rick. *Hardwiring Happiness: The New Brain Science of Contentment, Calm, and Confidence.* New York: Harmony, 2013.

Kabat-Zinn, Jon. *Full Catastrophe Living: Using the Wisdom of Your Body and Mind to Face Stress, Pain, and Illness.* Rev. ed. New York: Bantam, 2013.

Lantieri, Linda. *Building Emotional Intelligence: Techniques to Cultivate Inner Strength in Children.* Boulder, CO: Sounds True, 2008.

Schoeberlein, Deborah R., and Suki Sheth. *Mindful Teaching and Teaching Mindfulness: A Guide for Anyone Who Teaches Anything.* Somerville MA: Wisdom Publications, 2009.

Winston, Diana. *Wide Awake: A Buddhist Guide for Teens.* New York: Perigee Book, 2003.

Research

Jennings, P. A., and M. T. Greenberg. "The Prosocial Classroom: Teacher Social and Emotional Competence in Relation to Child and Classroom Outcomes." *Review of Educational Research, 79* (2009): 491–525.

Meiklejohn et al. "Integrating Mindfulness Training into K–12 Education: Fostering the Resilience of Teachers and Students." *Mindfulness.* 2012.

Yoder, Nicholas. "Teaching the Whole Child: Instructional Practices That Support Social-Emotional Learning in Three Teacher Evaluation Frameworks." Rep. American Institutes for Research, Jan. 2014. http://www.gtlcenter.org/sites/default/files/TeachingtheWholeChild.pdf.

Audio

Gretz, Emily, Cleveland Wehle, and Steve Wolf. *Yoga Nidra for Kids of All Ages.* Washington DC: Awasz Publishing, 2012, compact disc.

Kabat-Zinn, Jon, *Guided Mindfulness Meditation Series 1.* Boulder, CO: Sounds True, 2005, compact disc.

Salzberg, Sharon, *Guided Meditations for Love and Wisdom.* Boulder, CO: Sounds True, 2009, compact disc.

Stryker, Rod, *Relax into Greatness with the Treasure of Yoga Nidra.* Carbondale, CO: Para Yoga, 2003, compact disc.

ACKNOWLEDGMENTS

> Whether we know it or not, we transmit the presence of everyone we have ever known, as though by being in each other's presence we exchange our cells, pass on some life force and then we go on carrying that other person in our body, not unlike the springtime when certain plants in fields we walk through attach their seeds in the form of small burrs to our socks, our pants, our caps, as if to say, "Go on, take us with you, carry us to root in another place." —**NATALIE GOLDBERG**

When I first came across these words from Natalie Goldberg, it felt as if someone had reached deep down into my heart and turned the light switch on. We live on in each other, and every interaction, small or large, means something. This is why mindfulness is so important—it not only gives us tools to actually be alive and present during those encounters but it inspires us to make the most out of each and every moment so that we are truly living life as if it matters.

There are countless individuals who've inspired my work as a mindful educator who are not only part of my global, spiritual family, but part of me. I bow in deep gratitude to Venerable Thich Nhat Hanh (Thay), and his loving, gentle, and transformative teachings on mindfulness. Dharmacharya Shantum Seth for bringing Thay to India, Sister Chau Nghiem, Brother Phap Dung, and the entire Plum Village community for their support. Jon and Myla Kabat-Zinn for their encouragement, leadership, and wisdom. Deborah Schoberlein for her unwavering support. Richard and Catherine Frazier for their guidance and mentorship. Daniel Rechtschaffen and the Mindful Education Institute community; Richard Brady and the Mindfulness in Education Network board of directors; Mind and Life Summer Research Institute faculty (2011); the UMASS Medical School's Center for Mindfulness staff. Theo Koffler and Mindfulness

Without Borders. The late Tom Little, Jenny Ernst, and the entire Park Day School community. Margaret Cullen and the Stanford School of Medicine Center for Compassion and Altruism Research and Education (CCARE) community. Adele Diamond and the Brain Development and Learning staff. Enlightened administrators, Barb Sirotin, Bob Hetzel, and the late Uwe Bagnato from the American Embassy School; Sherry McClelland from Graded American School in Brazil; Crystal Land, Carl Thiermann, and Karen Bradley from Head-Royce School. My original educators' sangha: Barb Hegranes, Gene Harrell, Adele Caemmerer, Kathy Zabinski, Jann Fling, Cheryl and Jeff Perkins, Meemie Kemper, Lauren Alderfer, Anna and Michael Citrino, Sharon Lowen, and Dave and Jill Windahl. His Holiness the Karmapa. Professor Ramchandra Gandhi and our Delhi philosophy group. Satish Kumar and Schumacher College. Krishan Patel and the entire Service Space community. Kevin Hawkins and the MindWell Foundation. All of my colleagues in the Oakland Unified School District, especially the Social Emotional Learning and Leadership Development Team, Kristina, Mary, and Sonny. Collaborative for Academic Social and Emotional Learning friends, Ann McKay Bryson, Chris Hiroshima, and Linda Lantieri. Rachel Neumann, Hisae Matsuda, Nancy Fish, Terri Saul, and the entire Parallax Press team for asking me to write this book and working with me along the way. Thank you to my loving family, my parents, Amma (Vijaya), Appa (Rini), and my brother, Mani, for always believing in me. Much gratitude to my mother-in-law, Reiko, for her enthusiastic support and my father-in-law, Dr. Mark Wimbush, for his thorough editing and feedback. My beloved Chihiro—my partner in the practice of mindfulness and my partner for life. Most importantly I thank all of my students from the bottom of my heart—all of you are my greatest teachers.

ABOUT THE AUTHOR

© Polly Hommel

Meena Srinivasan, MA, National Board Certified Teacher, is an Indian American international educator and thought leader in the field of mindfulness in education. A contributor to United Nations' publications on inclusive education, she was one of the youngest educators to be awarded the prestigious National Board Certification by the United States National Board for Professional Teaching Standards. Srinivasan earned a master's degree in education from the University of California, Berkeley, and a bachelor's degree in history and political science from Amherst College. Her international outlook on education was enhanced by spending her junior year studying abroad at the London School of Economics. She has taught middle and high school students in Brazil, India, and California and currently works for the Oakland Unified School District's Social Emotional Learning and Leadership Development team.

Srinivasan is a student of Thich Nhat Hanh and was involved in the creation of his bestselling book *Planting Seeds: Practicing Mindfulness with Children*. She serves on the board of directors of the Mindfulness in Education Network, was core faculty of the Mindful Education Institute, and served on the advisory board of the San Francisco Asian Art Museum's exhibit, Yoga: The Art of Transformation. Meena's also a recipient of the Hemera Foundation's Contemplative Education Fellowship. She blogs about mindfulness based social emotional learning at http://teachbreathelearn.com/.

Meena lives in the San Francisco Bay Area with her husband, Eurasian American Filmmaker, Chihiro Wimbush. Bringing together their passion for education, media, mindfulness, and social justice, Meena and Chihiro started A Lens Inside, a fiscally sponsored project of United Charitable Programs—a registered 501(c)(3) public charity. A Lens Inside develops multimedia and films to create curriculum and educational programs that promote social emotional learning through the exploration of social issues. For more information, visit http://alensinside.org/.

RELATED TITLES

Anh's Anger by Gail Silver

Awakening Joy by James Baraz and Shoshana Alexander

Child's Mind by Christopher Willard

Everybody Present by Nikolaj Flor Rotne and Didde Flor Rotne

A Handful of Quiet by Thich Nhat Hanh

Is Nothing Something? by Thich Nhat Hanh

Planting Seeds by Thich Nhat Hanh

Steps and Stones by Gail Silver

Parallax Press is a nonprofit publisher, founded and inspired by Zen Master Thich Nhat Hanh. We publish books on mindfulness in daily life and are committed to making these teachings accessible to everyone and preserving them for future generations. We do this work to alleviate suffering and contribute to a more just and joyful world.

For a copy of the catalog, please contact:

Parallax Press
P.O. Box 7355
Berkeley, CA 94707
Tel: (510) 525-0101
www.parallax.org